THE FORMATION OF THE NEW TESTAMENT

YOUR
NO-NONSENSE
GUIDE TO
UNDERSTANDING
ITS AUTHENTICITY
AND CREDIBILITY

CHUCK GIANOTTI

ECS MINISTRIES
The Word to the World

The Formation of the New Testament: Your No-Nonsense Guide to Understanding Its Authenticity and Credibility

Chuck Gianotti

Published by:
ECS Ministries
PO Box 1028
Dubuque, IA 52004-1028
phone: (563) 585-2070
email: ecsorders@ecsministries.org
website: www.ecsministries.org

First Printed 2010

ISBN 978-1-59387-114-7

Copyright © 2010 ECS Ministries

Cover image: John Rylands fragment, P^{52}. The front cover image is a portion of John 18:31-33; the back cover image is a portion of John 18:37-38, c.a. early 2nd century. Used by permission of the John Rylands University Library at the University of Manchester, England.

For more literature to help in your spiritual growth and service for the Lord, visit the Bible-Equip website at *www.bible-equip.org*.

All rights reserved. No part of this publication may be reproduced or transmitted in any manner, electronic or mechanical, including photocopy, recording, or any information storage and retrieval system including the Internet without written permission from the publisher. Permission is not needed for brief quotations embodied in critical articles and reviews.

All Scripture quotations, unless otherwise indicated, are taken from the New American Standard Bible, Copyright © 1960, 1962, 1963, 1968, 1971, 1972, 1973, 1975, 1977, 1995 by The Lockman Foundation. Used by permission.

Printed in the United States of America

TABLE OF CONTENTS

Forward 5
Read This First! 7
  1. Introduction to the Issue 11
  2. The Need for Credibility 19
  3. An Historical Overview of the Resources 25
  4. Apostolic Authority of the Gospel 33
  5. Apostolic Authority of Acts and the Letters 49
  6. Influencing the Spread 59
  7. The Apostolic Fathers 71
  8. The Later Church Fathers 77
  9. The Non-Canonical Writings 89
  10. The Canon and Church Authority 101
  11. Formatting the Texts 107
  12. Putting It All Together 113
  13. What Difference Does It Make? 123
  14. Conclusion 127
Postscript: Faith & History 129
Glossary 133
Annotated Bibliography 137
Endnotes 141

"All Scripture is inspired by God and profitable for teaching,
for reproof, for correction, for training in righteousness;
so that the man of God may be adequate,
equipped for every good work."

2 Timothy 3:16-17

Forward

Theologian J. I. Packer was right when he said: "The problem of authority is the most fundamental problem that the Christian church ever faces." Understanding the process, standards, and history of canonization strengthens one's confidence in the authority of the Scriptures and equips one to defend it. *The Formation of the New Testament* is carefully researched, well written, and helpfully indexed. Chuck Gianotti gives us a useful tool for students, parents, and Bible teachers, as well as for those examining the Christian faith.

–Dr. Bill McRae, President Emeritus,
Tyndale University College and Seminary in Toronto

READ THIS FIRST!

The Christian faith rises or falls on the historical credibility of the Bible, particularly the New Testament writings. Are they historically plausible? Are they authoritative? How did the early Christians identify which books were inspired by God and which were not? How do we know they were right?

In our post-modern world, the very foundation for having this discussion has taken a beating. How can we know *anything* is true? Who defines what it means when we say something is true? Or for that matter, does it even *matter* what is true?

Every religion has its sacred documents, so what is so special about the Bible? Post-modern thinkers would tell us today that all religions can be true, as long as we understand that truth is a sociologically conditioned concept. The idea is that one sacred document is true for one person, while another sacred document is true for another ("true" in the sense that those documents provide comfort and meaning to their respective adherents). They are not necessarily true in the sense of historically accurate, we are told. But they are a different kind of true—a religious, spiritual kind of true. So for many people today the question of this book in your hands is really a moot issue. Why, then, this book?

> **The Christian faith rises or falls on the historical credibility of the Bible.**

We believe a document or a writing needs to be taken on its own terms and examined for what it really teaches and reflects about the world. In the case of the Bible, the New Testament has been held to the highest standard for most of its history. It has been viewed as historically true in the sense that it purports to be written by eyewitnesses of Jesus Christ and their immediate associates. Furthermore, the writings that compose the New Testament, when taken on their own terms and not passed through the post-modern interpretive lens, base the teaching they contain on historically factual events, most centrally the resurrection of Jesus Christ. We are told by many present-day scholars that this was a religious construct devised over a period of years to frame the decided impact that the humble carpenter of Nazareth had on the world. The myth, we are told, grew to the point of religious dogma. If this is true (that this is an accurate historical description of what happened), then Christianity is built on a religious fable.

The documents themselves don't allow that interpretation, for in the first letter to the Corinthians, the text says:

> "But if there is no resurrection of the dead, not even Christ has been raised; and if Christ has not been raised, then our preaching is vain, your faith also is vain. Moreover we are even found to be false witnesses of God, because we testified against God that He raised Christ, whom He did not raise, if in fact the dead are not raised. For if the dead are not raised, not even Christ has been raised; and if Christ has not been raised, your faith is worthless; you are still in your sins. Then those also who have fallen asleep in Christ have perished. If we have hoped in Christ in this life only, we are of all men most to be pitied." (1 Cor. 15:13-19)

> **The exclusivity of biblical Christianity is based on the statements of Jesus as recorded in the New Testament gospel accounts.**

Clearly, based on the text's own criterion, it really *does* matter whether the text itself (in this case, the record of Christ's resurrection) represents historically true information, post-modernism notwithstanding. Further, the documents include other statements attributed to Jesus that are offensive to the religious pluralism of our western world. For example, according to the writer of the gospel of John, Jesus said, "I am the way, and the truth, and the life; no one comes to the Father but through Me" (John 14:6). The record of Jesus' sayings does not allow for the common idea that all religions lead to the same destination, that all teach essentially the same truths. The exclusivity of biblical Christianity is based on the statements of Jesus as recorded in the New Testament gospel accounts.

If, on the other hand, one asserts that Jesus was wrong in making such a statement, then the person making the assertion is guilty of making an absolute moral judgment on the founder of Christianity, demonstrating an intolerance that is anathema in our post-modern mindset.

The only alternative is to challenge the historical record and conclude that the New Testament is not an accurate record of what Jesus said. Scorn would not be too strong a term to describe the attitude of those who maintain this third view toward those who hold to the historical credibility and authority of the New Testament documents.

We can see from the above quoted texts that the study of the historical veracity and authenticity of the New Testament text is essential. For if it can be demonstrated that the documents are reliable in their record of the life and teachings of Jesus Christ, then no one can dismiss the Jesus of the Bible in order to embrace a "Jesus" more suitable to a post-modern faith.

Much has been written and debated concerning these questions, but most of the scholarship is hidden away in theological tomes and in a technical language far removed from the average person's comprehension. Much one-sided thinking is heralded in the media, with the impression that there is general agreement among thinking people and scholars that the New Testament is not really what it purports to be or what your parents believed about it. After all, they say, we live in an enlightened, post-modern age.

This book reduces the vast amount of information on this topic into an accessible and readable form for the non-scholar. The goal is to show the credibility and reliability of the New Testament documents. I envision three kinds of readers:

1) The average, intelligent individual who is not a Christian but who is seeking truth and a foundation for his or her life.

2) The average, intelligent Christian who wants to better equip him or herself for defending the New Testament Scriptures.

3) Seekers of spiritual truth who are enrolled or planning to enroll in college or university. They will particularly benefit from this study.

I am indebted to the many scholars and writers whose works have honored God and His communication to us, those who have labored behind closed doors studying the ancient documents and the history surrounding the early church. This indebtedness goes far beyond what I can adequately express here.

As with all things laid down in print, many people have provided invaluable support in helping this book make its way from ideas to reality. My thanks go to Dr. Bill McRae, President Emeritus, Tyndale College and Seminary in Toronto, for reviewing the manuscript and providing much encouragement. Dr. Dan Wallace, Professor of New Testament Studies, Dallas Theological Seminary, provided critical feedback and suggestions in the early stages of the manuscript that helped direct me to relevant resources—and that despite his busy schedule. Tony Barone has provided a great sounding board for all things theological and otherwise! One who first discipled me and inspired in me a commitment to the Word of God is Bob Lehman. His love for the Word proved to be contagious, and it is that love which prompted me to write this book. Ruth Rodger provide much needed editing on the earlier manuscripts—what a servant she has been! Also Mark Wainwright and the staff at ECS Ministries have been instrumental in the development of this book. Their editorial and publishing expertise has made this book a reality. Any errors, inaccuracies and shortcomings are the responsibility of the author, and I take full responsibility for them.

Most especially I thank my wife, Mary, who believed in me, patiently listened to my ramblings and ideas, reviewed the draft in its many stages, and most of all has encouraged me at every step of this writing experience.

To *God* be the glory!

Chuck Gianotti

CHAPTER ONE

Introduction† to the Issue

In the western world the Bible has held a unique status, being revered highly by most as an unparalleled and powerful book. Faithful Christians have embraced it as God's unique communication to humans, and as such, authoritative for life. However, things have changed and continue to change. Modern assaults on the Bible are increasing. This can be attributed to a variety of reasons, of which the following are samples.

The Growth of Religious Pluralism

There is a growing awareness in our western world of other "sacred" texts which non-Christian religions view as authoritative, for example, the Book of Mormon (Church of the Latter Day Saints), the Quran (Islam), and the Bhagavad-Gita (Hinduism). As a result, the Bible is seen simply as one of many inspirational texts in the pantheon of world religions in the global village.

Attacks on Christianity

Post-modern rejection of rationalism. Truth, in our post-modern world, is no longer moored to objective reality. The notion that the Bible can be seen in its historical framework as addressing truth and corresponding

---

† For those who would like more detail and supporting resources, see the end of the book for extensive endnotes.

to reality is dismissed. Following this mindset, what matters is not *what* a person believes, but *whether or not* a person believes. The *object* of faith is irrelevant; the efficacy of faith itself is what is paramount. This is tantamount to believing that a placebo can be just as effective as a genuine cure.

Anti-conservative bias. Criticism is directed against those who hold a conservative view of the Bible, because such a view is confused with those held by religious extremists (for example, militant "Christian" sects and Muslim extremists). This constitutes guilt by association, and unfortunately the perception is widespread.

The proliferation of conspiracy theories. Various conspiracy theories claim that the present collection of NT[†] writings is the result of political motivations and gender issues culminating in the 4th century at the Council of Nicaea. One example, the popular novel *The da Vinci Code* occupied a position on the New York Times best seller list for several years.

The assertions of modern liberal scholarship. Walter Bauer, writing in 1971, "saw the early church as marked by widespread pluralism that was eventually suppressed by the rise of Catholic orthodoxy. Since the present Canon reflects the ascendancy of the orthodox party, the question must be raised as to the legitimacy of the Canon as a norm for original Christianity."[1]

Dr. Harry Gamble, representing many scholars who have built upon Bauer's work, asserts: "The historical study of the NT has steadily undermined the traditional legitimations of the canon (e.g., that these writings were composed by the apostles, or that they are distinguished by their inspiration)."[2] William R. Famer refers to a proposal that certain books now included in the New Testament Canon be excluded (i.e. Revelation) and others be included (i.e. Gospel of Thomas).[3] The well-known "Jesus Seminar" project, composed of a select group of scholars, flatly rejects many portions of the canonical gospel record as fabrications added later by the church.[4]

Institutional/denominational drift. Denominations which were once conservative in holding to a high view of the Bible are now moving to and promoting a more liberal view. In some cases this is preceded by adopting non-orthodox theologies which cannot be sustained by a conservative

---

[†] For brevity's sake, the New Testament and Old Testament will be referred to as "NT" and "OT" respectively.

reading of Scripture. Thus, there is an increase in what some call justified theological "developments." In effect, new theologies are forcing a weak view of the Bible. Some of Paul's writings, for example, are suspect because of his perceived "anti-women bias" and are therefore considered to be either uninspired or unauthentic.

The rise of revisionist historical research. New theories of how to conduct historical research and how to understand what has happened in the past have raised questions about our previously held assumptions of what really did take place two thousand years ago, that is, during the time the Bible was written and shortly thereafter.

> The Roman Catholic/Protestant debate continues over the nature of the canonization process.

The Roman Catholic/Protestant Debate. The Roman Catholic/Protestant debate continues over the nature of the canonization process, including divergent perspectives on the status of the so-called Apocrypha or "deuterocanonical books." One author summarizes the situation well:

> "Protestant scholars have typically asserted that canonical literature has intrinsic and self-authenticating authority which impresses itself on the conscientious reader, whereas Catholic scholars have typically maintained that the canon derives its authority from official recognition by the church."[5]

Put in the form of a series of questions, conservative New Testament scholars Carson and Moo ask:

> "What is the relation between canon and authority? Which comes first, a book's canonical status or its functional authority? What is the relationship between the authority of the text and the authority of the ecclesiastical body that recognizes (some would say 'confer') its canonical status?"[6]

David Dunbar asks the cogent questions:

> "Is it [i.e. the NT canon of Scripture] *merely* an offspring of the church's later history, thereby testifying only to the wisdom (or foolishness!) of the early Christians in selecting and authorizing particular writings from its past? Alternatively, is the closed canon—even though not explicitly delineated in the apostolic

period or in the New Testament—yet properly seen as the logical and organic development of certain principles resident in the New Testament documents and in redemptive-historical events that brought the church into existence?"[7]

DEBATES ABOUT THE NT TODAY ARE NOT NEW

Early church period (1st to 4th century). Other books (than those in the accepted NT Canon) circulated among the early Christian communities. They enjoyed various levels of acceptance in different swaths of those communities. Many spurious texts began to circulate that falsely claimed apostolic authority. Pseudo-Christian movements such as Gnosticism surfaced, challenging orthodox Christianity with texts of their own.

The Reformation period (early 16th century, though its roots go back farther). The Roman Catholic monk Martin Luther and others within that Church renewed the struggle over a certain set of writings which had found varying degrees of support or rejection through the church's first 1,500 years. These writings are called by Protestants "the apocryphal books," but Roman Catholics refer to them as "the deuterocanonical books." The divide on this issue continues into the present.

The rise of "higher criticism" (beginning in the 19th century). Technically speaking, *higher criticism* deals with the historical, "objective" research into the origins of the Bible, its authors, and how it came to be what we have in our hands today. This is to be distinguished from *lower criticism* (or *textual criticism*), which studies how a given text may have changed through the years of copying down to the present day.

Various forms of higher criticism have evolved, including:

1) *Form criticism,* which attempts to discern the underlying oral sources that led to the composition of the NT writings.

2) *Source criticism,* which focuses on how those sources were used.

3) *Redaction criticism,* which analyzes the literary and theological purposes the author used to structure his accounts.

Most often these are applied to the study of the Gospels, but some aspects of these are applied to the study of the Epistles as well.

Higher criticism, while being a legitimate method for studying historic literature, can also be used to draw conflicting conclusions from the same set of historical facts. Originating in Germany, higher criticism has been used by many to assert that most of the NT was of later origin than the 1st century, and that the biblical writings reflected the beliefs of the faith community and its legends and myths which developed among the earlier Christians and were embellished in succeeding generations. Although conservative scholars reach different conclusions from the same historical facts, higher criticism as a study has been maligned because it has been used by some to undermine confidence in the NT.

THE NEED EXISTS FOR A SOLID FOUNDATION FOR THE CHRISTIAN FAITH

Where there is lack of confidence in the Bible being the inspired Word of God, Christian faith no longer has an objective foundation and Christians have no assurance that what they believe is really true. The ramifications for Christianity are, therefore, enormous. Indeed, if there can be demonstrated an Achilles heel in this whole matter, it would be the subject of canonization. If the NT text is not what it purports to be, then the Christian faith is no better than any other religious system, having no certain basis for a revelation from God.

> If the NT text is not what it purports to be, than the Christian faith is no better than any other religious system.

THE "CANON" EXPLAINED

The NT did not suddenly appear at some specific date in the 1st century as a composite of twenty-seven books and with God's immediately evident imprimatur. The crux of the whole issue, then, is: How we can be sure that the twenty-seven books which comprise the NT are really those writings and only those writings which God intended as His specific written communication to us?

The word *canon* comes from the Greek word for a "measuring reed," and therefore came to signify "rule" or "standard."[8] Carson and Moo summarize the use of this term:

> "In ecclesiastical usage during the first three centuries, it referred to the normative doctrinal and ethical content of Christian faith. By

the fourth century it came to refer to the list of books that constitute the Old and New Testaments. It is this latter sense that predominates today: the 'canon' has come to refer to the closed collection of documents that constitute authoritative Scripture."[9]

This book is an investigation into how the various separate writings came to be collected into an authoritative whole which we call the Canon. The challenge comes when it is realized that many other books and letters were excluded from the Canon. Is it possible that God intended some books to be included but which were mistakenly left out? And vice versa—were some books included that should have been omitted? Martin Luther was suspicious of the book of James, for example. And a book called The Shepherd of Hermas was treated by many of the early Christians as authoritative, but was eventually left out of the Canon—why?

The investigation into the Canon of Scripture is part of the overall study called Bibliology. This larger discipline deals with understanding how God's thoughts have been communicated to our minds (and ultimately to our hearts) through His Word, the Bible.

BIBLIOLOGY		
Revelation	God's mind	→ original writers' minds
Inspiration	Writers' minds	→ original texts
Canonization	Original texts	→ post-apostolic acceptance
Transmission	Accepted texts	→ manuscript copies (MSS)
Translation	MSS copies	→ contemporary lang. texts
Illumination	Contemp. texts	→ our minds / hearts

We cannot ultimately *prove* the Bible is from God, if by proof we mean scientific verification. Historical research is more of a study of credibility. To be sure, there is "subjective" proof in the effects the NT has in the lives of those who believe its contents. However, in the study of the Canon, we are attempting to look at the credibility of the NT documents from an historical perspective. We believe the historical evidence supporting the NT documents in terms of their authenticity and authority is far more conclusive than the arguments against them.

An Overview of This Study

This study will answer the following questions:

> ➢ What was the process for determining how the NT came into being?

> ➢ What did those who were closest to the original authors of the NT books say about their writings? NT scholar Bruce Metzger emphasizes:
>
>> "What the apostles wrote, and what they authorized, can be known in no other way, than by the testimonies of those who lived at the same time with them, and the tradition of those who succeeded them."[10]

> ➢ How did the earliest post-apostolic Christians determine which documents were authoritative? How sure can we be sure that their conclusions are right?

> ➢ Are the NT documents reliable in what they purport to be, namely the authoritative, written Word of God?

A matter of authenticity and authority

There have been three main views of the process of canonization, each of which sees the matter of authority differently. One view asserts that canonization was the process in which the early believers identified the books that *already* had divine authority. That is, God handed down authoritative books or pieces of literature and left it up to Christians to distinguish between those books and all the other writings in circulation in the early years of the church. This view has it that the church did not *confer* authority on the books, but simply *identified* what God endorsed as authoritative. Therefore the church does not have authority either over or alongside the Canon of the NT; rather, the NT has authority over the church.

A second view holds that the church had the authority to confer canonical (or authoritative) status on the NT documents. A writing was included or excluded based on the authority of the church in making it so. This view is held by the Roman Catholic Church and the Orthodox churches (variously identified with regions or countries, Eastern Orthodox, Greek Orthodox, Russian Orthodox, etc.). In this view the church, as seen in its historic tradition, is one of two sources of authority (Scripture being the other).[11]

A third view common today is a humanistic approach—that the church assigned authoritative status to certain books because of their demonstrated usefulness to the church. "Religious authority was not simply intrinsic to the documents themselves."[12] The collection was the result of human composition, nothing more and nothing less. Whatever the church does, in fact, defines the church and its writings. This view is distinguished from the previous one in that here the process is understood more in a human / sociological / communalogical sense, stripped of any actual divine authority.

We believe that the most cogent view and that which is best supported by the evidence is the first view. God, as its divine Author, conferred authority by the very nature of His revelatory activity.

Chapter Two

The Need for Credibility

This study of canonicity is part objective and part subjective; it is also part history and part theology. Biblical scholars and historians come at the same data, make their extrapolations and draw implications, and then arrive at different conclusions. None can escape their particular bias. Words abound, like "plausible," "reasonably," and "inferred."[13]

However, the ramifications of this study beg us not to wallow in uncertainty. If the Bible is not what it presents itself to be, then it is just another religious book and nothing in it can be considered reliable, and by its own testimony Christians are "to be pitied" for what it teaches on things such as the bodily resurrection of Jesus Christ (1 Cor. 15:19). Yet, if the Bible *is* what it presents itself to be, the stakes are indeed momentous—God has spoken.

Historical Importance of the NT

The NT has been venerated for nearly two thousand years. It is commonly thought in the western world that the Bible (OT and NT) has been the most influential book of all time. In fact, the Bible is the authoritative Scripture for the largest religion in history. These facts should cause us to delve into this study carefully and with all seriousness.

> The NT has been venerated for nearly two thousand years.

The NT's Internal Claims of Authority

The authoritative statements of Jesus

Jesus is quoted in the canonical NT as making claims which, if true, are of eternal importance—and, if false, are preposterously deceptive. He is purported in Scripture to claim that the quality of a person's life absolutely depends on whether he or she follows His teachings:

> "Therefore everyone who hears these words of Mine and acts on them, may be compared to a wise man who built his house on the rock. And the rain fell, and the floods came, and the winds blew and slammed against that house; and yet it did not fall, for it had been founded on the rock. Everyone who hears these words of Mine and does not act on them, will be like a foolish man who built his house on the sand. The rain fell, and the floods came, and the winds blew and slammed against that house; and it fell—and great was its fall." (Matt. 7:24-27)

> "Heaven and earth will pass away, but my words will not pass away." (Matt. 24:35)

If Jesus did in fact say these things, then He was, in the sentiment of C. S. Lewis, a deceiver, delusional, or Lord—and if Lord, then we had better listen to Him!

The Bible's own claim of divine inspiration

> "All Scripture is inspired by God and profitable for teaching, for reproof, for correction, for training in righteousness; so that the man of God may be adequate, equipped for every good work." (2 Tim. 3:16-17)

While the context of these verses refers primarily to OT Scriptures, Peter considered Paul's writings to also be Scripture (see 2 Peter 3:15-16). And Peter reveals a high regard for Scripture:

> "But know this first of all, that no prophecy of Scripture is a matter of one's own interpretation, for no prophecy was ever made by an act of human will, but men moved by the Holy Spirit spoke from God." (2 Peter 1:20-21)

The Bible as we have it today warns about serious consequences for tampering with it. Consider the book of the Revelation, for example, where the writer says of his tome:

> "I testify to everyone who hears the words of the prophecy of this book: if anyone adds to them, God will add to him the plagues which are written in this book; and if anyone takes away from the words of the book of this prophecy, God will take away his part from the tree of life and from the holy city, which are written in this book." (Rev. 22:18-19)[14]

Thus, from this sampling of passages, the NT's testimony to its own importance needs to be seriously considered.

THE NT'S CLAIM TO ITS OWN HISTORICITY

The author of 1 John claims to be a personal eyewitness of things that he records:

> *John claims to be a personal eyewitness of things that he records.*

> "What was from the beginning, what we have heard, what we have seen with our eyes, what we have looked at and touched with our hands, concerning the Word of Life—and the life was manifested, and we have seen and testify and proclaim to you the eternal life, which was with the Father and was manifested to us—what we have seen and heard we proclaim to you also, so that you too may have fellowship with us; and indeed our fellowship is with the Father, and with His Son Jesus Christ. These things we write, so that our joy may be made complete." (1 John 1:1-4)

The author of 2 Peter writes as an eyewitness and appeals to his readers on this basis:

> "For we did not follow cleverly devised tales when we made known to you the power and coming of our Lord Jesus Christ, but we were eyewitnesses of His majesty. For when He received honor and glory from God the Father, such an utterance as this was made to Him by the Majestic Glory, 'This is My beloved Son with whom I am well-pleased'—and we ourselves heard this utterance made from

heaven when we were with Him on the holy mountain." (2 Peter 1:16; see also 1:10-12)

The writings of Luke (The Gospel According to Luke and The Acts of the Apostles) claim to be accurate historical records. The author shows remarkable historical keenness, having done careful research and interviews with eyewitnesses:

> Luke shows remarkable historical keenness, having done careful research and interviews with eyewitnesses.

> "Inasmuch as many have undertaken to compile an account of the things accomplished among us, just as they were handed down to us by those who from the beginning were eyewitnesses and servants of the word, it seemed fitting for me as well, having investigated everything carefully from the beginning, to write it out for you in consecutive order, most excellent Theophilus; so that you may know the exact truth about the things you have been taught." (Luke 1:1-4, see Acts 1:1-3)

Sir William Ramsay, after years of archeological research in Asia Minor, concluded:

> "Luke is a historian of the first rank; not merely are his statements of fact trustworthy, he is possessed of the true historic sense . . . in short, this author should be placed along with the very greatest of historians."[15]

The apostle Paul appealed to historical events and to the testimony of eyewitnesses that could be verified by his contemporaries:

> "For I delivered to you as of first importance what I also received, that Christ died for our sins according to the Scriptures, and that He was buried, and that He was raised on the third day according to the Scriptures, and that He appeared to Cephas, then to the twelve. After that He appeared to more than five hundred brethren at one time, most of whom remain until now, but some have fallen asleep; then He appeared to James, then to all the apostles; and last of all, as to one untimely born, He appeared to me also." (1 Cor. 15:3-8)

The writer of Hebrews appealed to eyewitness sources that conveyed the accounts of the life and teachings of Christ:

"How will we escape if we neglect so great a salvation? After it was at the first spoken through the Lord, it was confirmed to us by those who heard, God also testifying with them, both by signs and wonders and by various miracles and by gifts of the Holy Spirit according to His own will." (Heb. 2:3-4)

We can not escape the conclusion that the NT documents without doubt assert their own historical veracity. If they are not historically accurate or authentic, then the documents lose credibility. It would follow, then, that the NT documents are not worthy of the faith and trust which millions of people through the ages have placed in them; these people have all been duped! If, on the other hand, those documents are in fact credible and accurate, then God has spoken through Jesus Christ and His apostles. And He continues to speak definitively and absolutely in our post-modern world. The ramifications are, indeed, enormous!

> We can not escape the conclusion that the NT documents without doubt assert their own historical veracity.

A Theological Perspective

While the credibility of the NT documents is central to us today, some have argued that the idea of a closed collection of NT documents was foreign to the apostles and the 2nd century church. In fact, they say, the works of the apostolic fathers did not contain the concept of a NT Canon, much less a closed one. However, as Dunbar points out[16], the very idea of a definitive collection of authoritative documents is historically well grounded in four crucial factors:

1) The NT authors—as well as Jesus—viewed the OT as a closed corpus of inspired revelation, which would naturally lead to a similar concept for writings pertaining to the new covenant.

2) Jesus himself set His authority over against the teachers of His day with such statements as, "You have heard it said . . . but I say . . ." His "I am" statements are particularly pointed in portraying Him as God's present-day revelation. Bearing in mind that the teachings of Jesus formed the core of the new revelation, the early church was quite prepared for a new set of writings that would be authoritative on the level of the OT.

3) "The authority of Jesus for the early church was inseparable from the authority of the apostles. The word and work of Christ formed the 'canon' of the first believers, but as part of that work Jesus himself established the means, the formal authority, by which what was seen and heard in the fullness of time was to be transmitted and communicated."[17] (See Mark 3:14, Acts 10:39-42, Luke 10:16, Matthew 16:18, etc.) This is not circular reasoning, in that the early church relied on most of the NT documents to form its perspective on the concept of Canon.

Herman Ridderbos says, "With the passing of time and the church spreading over the whole world, the apostles could only keep written contact with the churches. And with the death of the apostles, oral tradition diminished in certainty and became less trustworthy, so that the written fixation of the apostolic tradition naturally acquired more significance."[18]

4) The rise of false teaching, of which Jesus himself warned (Matt. 7:15, 24:11, Mark 13:22, etc.) and also the apostles warned (1 John 4:1, 2 Peter 2:1), encouraged a definitive collection of authoritative writings that would identify orthodox teaching and truth. At this juncture, some skeptics like to quote Walter Bauer, who was the first to define "orthodoxy" as being merely a tag for the winners of the political and theological battles of the early church.[19] He says that the NT documents themselves were the result of the winners' theological perspective on things. In contrast to this is the clear fact that the NT documents which were accepted early on (here we are thinking of the gospel accounts as will be seen below), present the recognition of the difference between what is true and false teaching—and this predated the doctrinal controversies of the second and subsequent centuries.

So we see on numerous levels that the need for and the justification of a closed collection of recognized and accepted authoritative texts for the growth and nurture of the Christian movement was quite reasonable and to be expected.

CHAPTER THREE

AN HISTORICAL OVERVIEW OF THE RESOURCES

The early church based everything it knew about Jesus on what was conveyed to it by apostolic authority. Jesus did not personally pen any of the Christian Scriptures. The early church believed that some of the apostles and a few individuals closely associated with them wrote about the teaching and life of Jesus and also added other teachings. These writers carried what is termed *apostolic authority*. That is why the early believers "were continually devoting themselves to the apostles' teaching" (Acts 2:42). This was not to set the apostles' teachings over against the teachings of Jesus; the core of the apostles' teachings was, in fact, the teachings of Jesus.

> The early church based everything it knew about Jesus on what was conveyed to it by apostolic authority.

After the apostles died, some believers, particularly those who personally knew one or more of the apostles, still retained in their memory their teaching, called *apostolic tradition*. In time these apostolic acquaintances also died, but the apostolic tradition continued on, though with some tension. Other writings began to appear which claimed apostolic origin. In addition, the teachings handed down from the apostles were quickly challenged by groups that taught different doctrines.

The need for delineating between that which was authoritative for Christian life and teaching (that is, of genuine apostolic tradition) and that which was not became important. However, since the apostles and those who knew them were no longer alive, all that was left were the written documents and oral teachings which were being passed down over a few generations. As we all know, the faculty of human memory is not always reliable, so who, then, decided which competing books were authentic? And how did the early (post-apostolic) generations of believers keep the true teachings of Christ and the apostles alive after they were all gone?

The "problem" today is compounded by the fact that we are hundreds of years removed from the process and have only some of the written documents containing what the early generations of Christians believed that led to the establishment of the Canon. But that is the core of the challenge today: how did the early church resolve the issue, and can we consider what it did credible?

> How did early generations of believers keep the true teachings of Christ and the apostles alive after they were all gone?

Actually, the first list of authoritative books was comprised of exactly the twenty-seven books of the NT that we now have. It was assembled relatively late by Athanasius in AD 367, though it is not clear that this list was universally endorsed. But what happened from the death of the apostles until that time?

Modern scholarship raises serious questions about even the idea of a definitive collection of books to be considered Scripture. Gamble writes:

> "There is no intimation at all that the early Church entertained the idea of Christian scriptures, much less a collection of them . . . the passage of time, the demise of the apostles, and the dissipation of oral tradition both led to the composition of Christian writings and elevated their importance as a means of sustaining the Church's relationship to the decisive events of its origins."[20]

It is probably true that the eschatological hope of the first generation of Christians was such that there was probably little thought of providing an enduring collection of writings for future generations. But can it be sustained that there was never such a thought in the *subsequent* generations of Christianity? We believe, as will be seen below, that indeed the subsequent generations of Christians placed great value on apostolic writings following the deaths of the Twelve and the apostle Paul. In time, the concept of the Canon arose simply out of necessity.

An Approach

As noted above, the author of The Gospel According to Luke showed evidence of being a true historian. He identified what appears to be a three stage development in the preservation of the life and teachings of Christ. (Luke 1:1-4)

Oral tradition: This is the teaching orally "handed down to us" by "eyewitnesses and servants of the word." Included in this would be firsthand verbal accounts by the apostles of the life and teachings of Christ, as well as the "sayings of Christ" that circulated through word-of-mouth by teachers and preachers.[21]

Written tradition: There were also written sources Luke consulted: "many [who] have undertaken to compile an account."

Purposeful ordering of the events: Finally, Luke sorted through the data and rendered a written account with the express goal of affirming the faith of his reader, Theophilus.

The Historical Documents

What we DO NOT have

Obviously, we do not have the original writers or witnesses or audio/video recordings of their teachings.[22] Neither do we have the original documents of the NT or original ancillary documents (those written by the immediately succeeding generations of Christians).

The original autographs were penned using primitive materials such as parchments and leather, all of which were subject to deterioration with handling and climate conditions. Each written gospel or epistle would have been eagerly sought and passed around from church to church, which would have ensured further degradation of the material. Most likely, copies would have been made to facilitate their circulation with no thought to venerating the originals. Some have speculated that God knew we would have tended to worship those originals documents as religious relics, so He prevented them from being preserved.[23]

What we DO have

We have extant *copies* of the original documents and writings (plus citations and translations from ancient times) of early Christians, both in their entirety and in fragments. By *extant* we mean that an ancient document has survived to the present day. These actual manuscript copies are currently stored in museums, libraries, and monasteries around the world. Once the writings were recognized as of enduring significance, the early Christians became prolific in copying them. These copies are called *manuscripts*, or MSS.

About five thousand hand-written Greek manuscripts exist today that date from the 2nd century through the Middle Ages.[24] Some of these are mere fragments, but many are complete copies.[25] There are, in addition, about eight thousand various versions, that is, translations from ancient times.

The earliest fragment dates to the first half of the 2nd century. It is called P[52], from the John Rylands collection in Manchester, England, and contains a small portion of John's gospel.

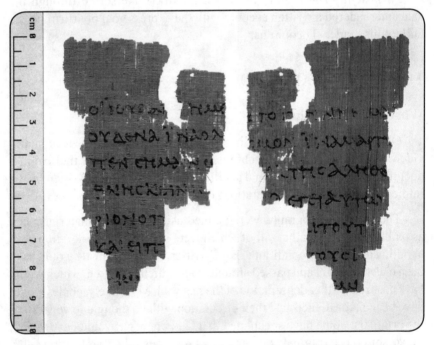

Figure 1. John Rylands fragment, P[52]. The left image is a portion of John 18:31-33, the right (backside) is a portion of John 18:37-38, c.a. early 2nd century. Used by permission of the John Rylands University Library at the University of Manchester, England.

The oldest surviving fragment of Paul's writings, the Chester Beatty manuscript, P[46] dates from AD 200. The earliest *complete* manuscript of the NT surviving to this day is the Codex Sinaiticus[26] (a.k.a. "Aleph" or "A") dated ca. 4th century.

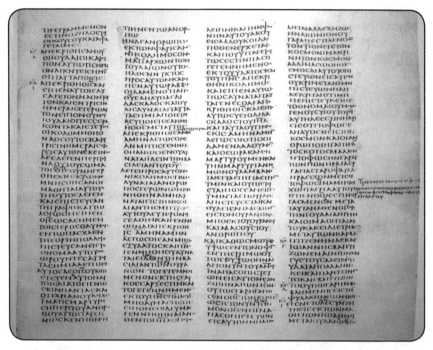

Figure 2. Codex Sinaiticus, Gospel of John 2:17-3:24. Owned by the British Library, London. Used by permission of the Center for the Study of New Testament Manuscripts. Notice the correction in the right column, evidently placed there by an ancient scribe!

Another early manuscript is the Codex Vaticanus (a.k.a. "B" or "03"). It is so named because it is housed in the Vatican Library and has been there since its existence became known. It is believed to have been written in the 4th century just before the Codex Sinaiticus, but some pages are missing that contain portions of the NT. Its origin is debated, the main suggestions being either Rome or Egypt, with some thinking Asia Minor.[27]

In addition to manuscript copies of the canonical texts, we also have over two thousand lectionaries extant. *Lectionaries* are works containing biblical materials arranged for reading according to the sequences of the ecclesiastical calendar.[28] These often aided in church services in early times.

They contain quotes from, and allusions to, the NT writings, much like lectionaries currently in use in some churches today.

Finally we have copies of writings of the post-apostolic writers containing what they thought and taught *about* the various writings in circulation that claimed apostolic authority. The earliest of these writings, commonly called *the Apostolic Fathers*, bridge the gap between the time of the apostles and subsequent generations of Christians. These authors were considered to be part of the generation that had personal knowledge of the apostles. In general they wrote from the latter portion of the 1st century and into the 2nd century. Among the more well known of these writings are those of Ignatius, Clement, and Polycarp. Some of the writings, like the Didache, are known only by the title of the book.

> To understand how the collection of NT books came into being, we must understand what the apostolic fathers said and thought about these matters.

Clearly, to understand how the collection of NT books came into being, we must understand what the apostolic fathers said and thought about these matters. Most of what we know of their thinking comes from the work of the well-known historian Eusebius writing in the 4th century, who preserved many of the writings of those early writers. "A principle source for establishing the canonical view of the early church is the Ecclesiastical History of Eusebius of Caesarea (AD 260-340), whose own position is deeply indebted to two Alexandrian Fathers (Clement and Origen)."[29] Clearly, without his historical work our knowledge of the church in the centuries immediately following the apostolic times would be greatly impoverished.

Following the apostolic fathers was a long line of writers which includes such authors as Irenaeus, Justin Martyr, and Tertullian. These *church fathers* generally followed the apostolic fathers and included apologists and theologians through the first five centuries of the church. A great number of their writings have survived to the present day. From these sources we are able to garner quotes and allusions that help substantiate the existence of—and in some cases the authority of—various apostolic books in circulation. In these writings, we also find discussions and determinations by writers or records of the councils concerning the various documents in question.[30]

Conclusion

Despite the lack of *original* documents, we do have a plethora of ancient documents that can help us reconstruct the process of canonization. More than any ancient book, the NT documents are well represented in the historical source material, and are more than adequate for determining the genuineness and integrity of the Canon.

Chapter Four

Apostolic Authority of the Gospel

From the earliest historical writings, the apostles were held in great esteem and their teachings taken as authoritative. The reason for this stance was the understanding that the apostles knew Christ personally and were, therefore, valid and official witnesses for the purpose of relaying His actual teachings. Since Jesus did not leave any personally written documents, NT scholar F. F. Bruce states,

> "Those whose apostleship was recognized by fellow-Christians were acknowledged to be Christ's agents, speaking by His authority. Their interpretation of the OT writings was therefore, in practice, as binding as those writings."[31]

We therefore begin our investigation of the Canon with a look at the four canonical gospels. Simply put, these were accepted by the earliest believers as authentic biographies of Jesus Christ.

Historical Uniqueness of the Canonical Gospels

Until modern times, the four-fold canonical gospels have been held to be genuine and uniquely apostolic, that is, the sole authoritative records of the life of Christ. Present-day scholarship has called this into question.

Some, such as Harry Gamble, claim that while the four gospels attained clear prominence by the late 2nd century, their preeminence was neither universal nor exclusive. Gamble goes on to assert that the preponderance of other "gospels" which drew upon and modified the same sources as the four "indicates that in the first half of the second century the gospel accounts which we know as canonical were not recognizably unique and had not acquired special authority." It is contended that new gospels continued to be composed through much of the 2nd century and that other gospels were referred to by Christian writers of the 2nd century besides the four. "At least their availability did not inhibit the ongoing production of similar documents." Gamble claims that "the currency of so many gospel accounts also shows that the eventual development of a collection of only four gospels was the result of a selective process."[32]

> Manuscript evidence for the four canonical gospels is well attested as being no later than the middle of the 2nd century.

Gamble's viewpoint is popular, especially in religious studies on university campuses. However, this sweeping mischaracterization of the historical data is unwarranted on many fronts.

First, the dating of those other "gospels" is not clear as to which or whether any of them originated in the first half of the 2nd century. On the other hand, manuscript evidence for the four canonical gospels of Matthew, Mark, Luke, and John is well attested as being no later than the middle of the 2nd century. And we would argue there is good evidence for a 1st century composition of these four (see below).

The lack of inhibition for producing other gospels does not speak against the acceptance and uniqueness of the four canonical ones. In fact, if Paul's writings are taken as authentic, Christians are warned in Galatians 1:8-9 and elsewhere that false teaching would arise. Paul even uses the word "gospel" to describe their teaching. The currency of so many "other" gospels could lead to a different conclusion—there were many imitators that arose subsequently to the four who wanted to give the early Christian movement a push in a different direction. Modern liberal scholars are not convincing in their arguments.

ORAL TRADITION: THE "SAYINGS OF JESUS"

So, then, after Jesus ascended back to heaven, how did the process of preserving His teachings begin? The earliest circulation of Jesus' teachings was by oral transmission, that is, word-of-mouth. The apostles naturally conveyed the teachings of Christ as they traveled around.

Since there was obviously a limit to how many places the apostles themselves could go, there soon developed a collection of quotes that began to circulate as Christians relayed the apostles' message to others. This led to what is now called *the sayings of Jesus*. These can sometimes be seen in various post-apostolic writings where sayings of Jesus are quoted, but those sayings are not found in the canonical gospels. It is possible then that the "sayings of Jesus" included some things that are in the Gospels and also some things Jesus said that were not. However, these references are evidence that teachings attributed to Jesus were being passed along and were considered authoritative.

> The earliest circulation of Jesus' teachings was by oral transmission, that is, word-of-mouth.

It might be easy to think that much was distorted during this time of oral transmission. Remember the childhood game of Telephone? As the "secret" is whispered from one mouth to another's ear and goes around the circle, the message changes, sometimes drastically. Was the passing on of Jesus' teachings subject to the same nature of haphazard communication? Carson and Moo counter:

> "The importance of memorization in first-century Jewish society is undeniable, and we are justified in thinking that this provides a sufficient basis for the careful and accurate oral transmission of the gospel material. Recent study of eyewitness testimony in the Greco-Roman world at large also generally confirms the value and accuracy of such testimony. And when we add to these points the very real possibility that the words and actions of Jesus were being written down from the beginning, we have every reason to think that the early Christians were both able and willing to hand down accurately the deeds and words of Jesus."[33]

It is entirely possible that the apostles themselves may have taken some hand-written notes on Jesus' teachings during His earthly life and that they could easily have continued writing from memory after His resurrection. There is no good reason to object to this very real probability.

Papias, a disciple of the apostle John, placed high importance on the oral teachings of the apostles about Christ. Writing in the early part of the 2nd century, he says:

> "For I did not, like the multitude, take pleasure in those who spoke much, but in those who taught the truth; nor in those who related strange commandments, but in those who rehearsed the commandments given by the Lord to faith, and proceeding from truth itself. If, then, anyone who had attended on the elder came, I asked minutely after their sayings,—what Andrew or Peter said, or what was said by Philip, or by Thomas, or by James, or by John, or by Matthew, or by any other of the Lord's disciples: which things Aristion and the presbyter John, the disciples of the Lord, say. For I imagined that what was to be got from books was not so profitable to me as what came from the living and abiding voice."[34]

Some have suggested, therefore, that the oral tradition had greater weight than any written works of the apostles. They assert that later writings, like the Gospel of Thomas, contain parts of the oral tradition not included in the four canonical gospels.[35] However, that is to misunderstand Papias. Carson and Moo respond,

> "It has been convincingly argued that Papias magnifies the importance of oral tradition for his *commentary* on the words of the Lord, not for the actual content of those words . . . elsewhere Papias rushes to deny that there is any error in Mark's gospel . . . surely this would be a strange maneuver if Papias disparaged *all* written record"[36] (emphasis in the original).

Although it seems popular among many present-day scholars to assert that a long period of oral tradition transpired before anything was written down, this is not supported by the historical facts. "The world into which Jesus was born was highly literate."[37]

References to the "Fourfold Gospel"

The earliest records show written references to four gospels in the early 2nd century. Formally speaking, each of the canonical gospels is anonymous; that is, the authors do not identify themselves in the writings the way that, say, Paul does. But from the earliest times the names of Matthew, Mark, Luke, and John have been associated with them. In the early church, however, the four writings were not referred to as *four* separate accounts, but as *one* gospel, albeit "according" to Matthew, Mark, Luke, and John respectively.

There was, to be sure, much debate about the four gospel accounts. But the issue was not the question of *how many* authentic accounts there were; rather, the early believers wanted to understand *why* there were precisely *four*, and why they differed from each other.

> In the early church, the four writings were not referred to as *four* separate accounts, but as *one*.

One scholar objects by pointing out that "some old manuscripts contain only one Gospel," going on to say that various gospel accounts received individual support early on without support for the others. An example of this was the aberrant sect of Marcion (see below) which accepted only Luke or a form of Luke.[38] However, examples such as Marcion's list don't carry much weight, because his list of authoritative books was highly suspect, selecting only some of the writings (ten of Paul's letters and Luke's gospel) and rejecting other books which smacked of "legalism" (in his thinking) with references to the OT law (like James and some of Paul's writings). Books like Matthew were, therefore, because of their Jewish nature, rejected by Marcion, along with the rest of what became the canonical NT books (see below).

Some scholars claim that the four canonical accounts of Christ's life on earth were not accepted with absolute authority because of the "freedom" with which copyists made changes. In fact, there were many errors in copying the NT text, judging from the preponderances of the differences in the manuscripts. But to assert that these changes were due to theologically motivation is contrary to the facts. A better assessment is that the copyists, because they held certain texts in high regard, were concerned about the purity of the texts. The changes generally were not made for theological reasons, but rather to correct what they thought were errors in the copies.

The copyists maintained a great respect for the text and took great pains to get back to the original, the "correct" text—they were not challenging the text's authority. Even today there is great effort through textual criticism (see page 14) to determine as far as possible the original text of the canonical books of the NT. With a multitude of manuscripts, conservative belief is that the *original* documents are the authoritative writings, while the manuscripts relay that authority to the degree that they accurately represent the original texts. Copyist changes do not, therefore, reflect on the *authority* of the texts negatively, but rather on the accuracy of *transmission* of the texts.

Sampling of References

The following is a sampling of what the early writers had to say about these things.

Clement of Rome (AD 96) quotes the words of Jesus (Sermon on the Mount) as being on the prophetic level. For example:

> "The Holy Spirit saith, 'Let not the wise man glory in his wisdom, neither let the mighty man glory in his might, neither let the rich man glory in his riches; but let him that glorieth glory in the Lord, in diligently seeking Him, and doing judgment and righteousness,' [quote from Jeremiah 9:23] being especially mindful of the words of the Lord Jesus which He spake, teaching us meekness and long-suffering. For thus He spoke: 'Be ye merciful, that ye may obtain mercy; forgive, that it may be forgiven to you; as ye do, so shall it be done unto you; as ye judge, so shall ye be judged; as ye are kind, so shall kindness be shown to you; with what measure ye mete, with the same it shall be measured to you.'"[39]

Notice the parallel treatment: "The Holy Spirit saith . . ." and ". . . the Lord Jesus . . . spake . . ." This suggests that Clement treats the teachings of Jesus on the same level as OT Scripture, and therefore having similar authority.

In ***The Second Epistle of Clement***[40] ***to the Corinthians*** (2nd century), the writer refers frequently to sayings of Jesus with these words attached: "*as Scripture says*." While many scholars say this formula does not always mean the author believes the quote is from an "inspired" book, it is clear that the sayings of Jesus were circulating in written form and given some level of authority.[41]

The Epistle of Barnabas (AD 100-130) quotes sayings of Jesus with "*as it is written*," a common formula for introducing OT Scripture, suggesting that the writer viewed Jesus' teaching as authoritative, probably on the same level as the OT.

Polycarp (AD 110-120) used "*it is said in these Scriptures . . .*" to introduce Jesus' sayings. Clearly, the teachings of Jesus carried authority even if the question of inspiration remained unclear.

Justin Martyr (AD 150-165) was well acquainted with the gospels of Matthew and Luke, as well as probably Mark and John,[42] which he held in high regard and considered to be of apostolic origin.[43] Referring to his view of the gospel writings, Dunbar says, "The apostolic *Memoirs* are regarded most probably as equal in authority to the Old Testament prophets. This is supported by Justin's report that both the prophets and the Memoirs were read in the weekly worship services of the church."[44]

The Diatessaron (ca. AD 170), written by Tatian, was an attempt to weave the four gospel accounts into a single volume, and it apparently enjoyed wide acceptance among the churches. This gives substantial evidence to the awareness of the four gospel accounts as unique, well established, and authoritative by the latter part of the 2nd century—it was clear that these four accounts were the subject of harmonization. Obviously, they were well known long before this, and the chronological difficulties were also well known (just as they are today).

It is important also to note that there was no effort to modify the four gospel accounts among the churches aside from those movements which came to be seen as heretical. Gamble, however, along with others, asserts that Tatian's "free-handling of the text shows that he did *not* value these documents as individual—let alone sacrosanct writings but was interested only in their contents."[45] However, this argument is specious. Tatian was simply the first in a long line of individuals who have undertaken the effort to harmonize the gospels accounts, and this in no way reflects a low view of them. If Tatian really wanted to "freehand" the text, he could have modified them outright and removed the difficulties. The fact that he did not and that he used only these four accounts speaks of the high value he placed on them.

Irenaeus, writing around AD 180, was the first to formally argue for the exclusive authority of the four gospel accounts.[46] At one point he speaks of the apostolic writings, ". . . which are indeed perfect since they were spoken by the Word of God and his Spirit."[47] While some conclude that this means a late acceptance of the four accounts, another conclusion provides a better analysis of the historical facts: there simply was no need for an early defense of them because of their widespread acceptance and assumed authority from the beginning. When later "gospels" arose, and sects began to assert their writings to support aberrant doctrines, a defense became necessary. Because of this, the late defense of the gospels actually speaks more toward the acknowledged early acceptance them rather than later. Dunbar concludes, "It is evident, then, that Irenaeus used a body of authoritative literature whose lines conformed closely to our present canon."[48]

The Individual Gospel Accounts

According to Matthew

The earliest references to The Gospel According to Matthew assume its authority and authorship. In fact there is no evidence that any of the canonical gospels ever circulated *without* the designation "according to . . . ," in this case, Matthew.[49]

Papias[50] (AD 130-140) knew some of the apostles personally and is believed to have been a disciple of the apostle John. He writes that "Matthew put together the oracles [of the Lord] in the Hebrew language . . ."[51] Interestingly, there is no manuscript evidence that this gospel account was written in Hebrew; our earliest copies are all in Greek. It is entirely possibly that Papias was referring to the language of the Hebrew people, which at the time of the apostles was Greek (or Aramaic). Nevertheless, in Papias we have a second-generation Christian referring to a gospel account written by an author named Matthew. Since this Matthew is mentioned without further explanation, it must have been a well-known Mathew, both to the author and to his readers. There was no Matthew more well-known than the apostle Matthew, so the evidence strongly favors authorship by that apostle. In fact, the authorship was never questioned by the early Christian writers, the unanimous agreement being that Matthew, also known as Levi, one of the original twelve disciples of the Lord, was the writer.

> Determining the date an ancient document was written can be difficult.

Determining the date an ancient document was written can be difficult. Conservative scholars determine the approximate dates of a written document by considering various factors including:

1) The approximate dates of the earliest reference to that document.

2) References inside the document to historical events.

3) Specific comments by subsequent writers in the early church (for example, Eusebius).

Even then, sometimes agreement and certainty are difficult. The date of writing for Matthew's gospel is debated by most scholars, some placing it as late as AD 80-100 and a few as early as AD 60-66.[52]

According to Mark

The early Christians believed that John Mark (of Acts 13-16 fame) recorded the teachings of Peter concerning the life and teachings of Jesus. Papias (writing ca. AD 130-140), understood this to be the case:

> "Mark became Peter's interpreter and wrote down accurately all that he remembered, whether the sayings or the doings of the Lord, but not in order—for he had neither heard the Lord nor followed him, but followed Peter later on, as I said. Peter was accustomed to teach as occasion required, but not as though he were making a compilation of the dominical oracles. So Mark made no mistake in writing down certain things as he called them to mind; for he paid attention to one thing: to omit none of the things he had heard and to make no false statements in any of them."[53]

A few observations from the above quote are in order. The writing by Mark in question had to do with the life and teachings of "the Lord," obviously the Lord Jesus Christ. Although many commentators conjecture that Mark was present at the arrest of Jesus (Mark 14:51-52), he was not one of the official Christ-appointed witnesses and was most likely not an observer of Lord's life from the baptism on. So, being a close follower of Peter, his gospel heavily relied upon that apostle's teachings. Peter's teachings did not present the life of Christ in systematic or chronological order; Mark apparently sorted through Peter's teaching and organized the stories into a structured, written presentation. Papias emphasizes Mark's accuracy and carefulness. It follows that The Gospel According to Mark therefore systematized Peter's teachings on the life and teachings of Christ.

Clement of Alexandria (writing in the latter part of the 2nd century) wrote that Mark was sought by the followers of Peter to write down what Peter had said. Irenaeus (writing ca. AD 178) held that Mark recorded Peter's teachings:

> "After their [i.e., Peter and Paul's] departure, Mark, the disciple and interpreter of Peter, did also hand down to us in writing what had been preached by Peter."[54]

It could be said that these later writers (Clement and Irenaeus) simply repeated what Papias said; this would mean that they were not independent witnesses. While this is mere speculation, it would nonetheless still speak to the settled acceptance of Papias's report by the end of the 2nd century.

Although Irenaeus and Clement disagree on the precise circumstances of its composition, both agree that Mark's account was written in Rome. "If the author of the gospel was indeed John Mark, then references to him in the New Testament also place him in Rome."[55]

Because of his association with Peter, Mark's writings were considered authoritative. This is quite interesting in light of Mark's early failure in the work of the gospel (Acts 13-16) and Paul's later acceptance of him as "useful" (2 Tim. 4:11). Indeed, Mark became *very* useful, as borne out by the early church's acceptance of his recording of the gospel account.[56] Interestingly, Mark's close association with Peter is seen in 2 Peter 5:13, where the apostle refers to him as his "son" (in the faith).

The date of writing is considered to be around AD 57-59 (or as late as AD 70).

According to Luke

Luke was a frequent companion on Paul's missionary journeys[57], and he accompanied the apostle as far as his Roman imprisonment (Acts chapters 16–28). His account of the life of Christ reflects careful research, interviewing of many witnesses, and consulting of many sources (Luke 1:1-4). No doubt he was influenced greatly by Paul's teachings.

What did Paul know of the earthly life of Christ? If we hold to the historical reliability of the book of Acts and Paul's own writings, he had access to Peter and James and the rest of the apostles, as well as having spent some time with them at various junctures in his ministry (see, for example, Acts 11:30 and Galatians 1:18-19, 2:9-11). It was probable that during those times the other apostles filled him in on some details about Jesus' teaching.[58] While Paul did not receive the gospel message from the other apostles (Galatians chapters 1–2), it is unlikely that he would not appreciate and relish some of the details of Jesus' life and teaching conveyed by those who had witnessed them personally.

Paul alluded to the authority of Luke's gospel when in 1 Timothy 5:18 he linked a quote from Luke 10:7 with a quote from Deuteronomy 25:4 in the OT and introduced them both as "Scripture":[59]

> "For the Scripture says, 'You shall not muzzle the ox while he is threshing,' and 'The laborer is worthy of his wages.'" (1 Tim. 5:18)

"You shall not muzzle the ox while he is threshing." (Deut. 25:4)

"Stay in that house, eating and drinking what they give you; for the laborer is worthy of his wages. Do not keep moving from house to house." (Luke 10:7)

Irenaeus (about AD 178) understood Luke to be the follower of Paul who relayed the gospel that Paul preached. "Luke also, the companion of Paul, recorded in a book the gospel preached by him."[60]

Since Luke was written before Acts (see Acts 1:1-2) and Acts was written prior to Paul's death[61], The Gospel According to Luke must have had an early date of composition, which speaks for its authenticity. Luke probably wrote it in AD 60-61 (to the late 60s).

According to John

The gospel account according to John was originally accepted as authentic by the earliest Christians. However, the book later became controversial because of the Gnostics (see below) who used it to support their aberrant theological positions.

As with the other three gospels, this one also is formally anonymous (that is, the author is not identified internally to the writing). However the name of the author, just like the other canonical gospels, was attached as soon as the four began to circulate together as the "fourfold gospel." F. F. Bruce makes an interesting comment,

> **The gospel account according to John was originally accepted as authentic. However, the book later became controversial because of the Gnostics.**

> "It is noteworthy that, while the four canonical gospel accounts could afford to be published anonymously, the apocryphal gospel accounts which began to appear from the mid-second century onwards claimed (falsely) to be written by apostles or other persons associated with the Lord."[62]

The earliest fragmentary evidence of this gospel, as mentioned earlier, is P^{52} from the Rylands collection, dated ca. AD 130. The existence of the Diatessaron, a harmony of the four gospel accounts (written shortly after AD 165), required prior existence of all four accounts, including John.

Irenaeus, writing AD 182-188, said: "John, the disciple of the Lord, who also had leaned upon His breast, did himself publish a gospel during his residence at Ephesus in Asia."[63] Being personally acquainted with Polycarp, a disciple of the apostle John, Irenaeus also said this:

> "I remember the events of those days more clearly than those which have happened recently, for what we learn as children grows up with the soul and becomes united to it, so I can speak even of the places in which the blessed Polycarp sat and disputed, how he came in and went out, the character of his life, the appearance of his body, the discourse which he made to the people, how he reported his converse with John and with the others who had seen the Lord, how he remembered their words, and what were the things concerning the Lord which he had heard from them, including his miracles and his teaching, and how Polycarp had received them from the eyewitnesses of the word of life, and reported all things in agreement with the Scriptures."[64]

Since the composition date of John's gospel was later than the other three accounts, it is not surprising that the historical record shows its circulation beginning later than the other three. However, there was virtually universal acceptance of this gospel account by the end of the 2nd century.

The external evidence is conclusive for the authorship of The Gospel According to John being identified with John the apostle. However, Carson and Moo point out that:

> ". . . [the] large majority of contemporary scholars reject this view . . . much of their argument turns on their reading of the *internal* evidence. Nevertheless, it requires their virtual dismissal of the external evidence. . . . Most historians of antiquity, other than New Testament scholars, could not so easily set aside evidence as plentiful and as uniform."[65]

In other words, many today try to dismiss John's authorship of the gospel, contrary to solid historical research, because of how they read John's gospel itself from a purely literary analysis. Such an approach reveals an unhistorical predisposition that is unwarranted.

As for the internal evidence, many today assert, for example, that an unlearned fisherman from Galilee who lived most of his ministry life in Ephesus could not have had literary capability for being the author. While this may *seem* plausible on the surface, there are a number of good responses to the contrary. For one, there is no reason to believe John was illiterate. To be sure he was jeered by his detractors as an "untrained layman," as was Jesus (see Acts 4:13 and John 7:15). But coming from a prosperous family with a successful fishing business, he most likely could read and write well.[66]

If the apostle John was not the author, then why would the author have completely omitted any references to John the apostle by name? That would have been a monumental slight to "the disciple whom Jesus loved." A good explanation is lacking. On the other hand, if John was in fact the author, then modesty better explains his nameless self-references; he saw himself simply as that "disciple whom Jesus loved." This observation of internal evidence strongly supports the external evidence that John the apostle was indeed the author.

The probable date of writing for this gospel has been placed anywhere from AD 70 to later in the 1st century. Some suggest a date somewhere between AD 80 and 85.

THE SYNOPTIC "PROBLEM"

The word *synoptic* is used to describe three of the gospels, namely Matthew, Mark, and Luke, which have much material that is similar (and in some cases identical) in wording. Questions naturally arise: How do we account for the similarities? Did they copy from one another? Was there another document from which the synoptic writers borrowed? And since there are so many similarities, how then do we account for the differences?

An answer which satisfies some is that the many similarities can be explained by the Synoptic Gospels having the same *divine* Author. But while I believe that the Spirit of God inspired the writing of these accounts, this does not explain the mechanism by which God used human authors to pen narratives so similar and yet so different.

How do we explain the similarity of content?

The similarities, and in some cases identical wording, suggest either or both of two things at work:

1) One or more of the writers used the others' accounts as source material.

2) There was a common source of information upon which they all drew.

The suggestion that the gospel writers used sources should not undermine our confidence in their authority, especially in light of the fact that Luke himself admits to this practice; he states in Luke 1:1-4 that he researched various sources, including eyewitnesses.

A theory has been suggested and is commonly held that a now lost document (commonly called "Q") existed which contained sayings of Jesus from which all three (or at least two) drew. The fact that we have no manuscript evidence of such a document has caused some to be suspicious

> The suggestion that the gospel writers used sources should not undermine our confidence in their authority.

of this suggestion.[67] However, despite some difficulties, this theory seems to make sense of the similarities. If in fact there was such a document as "Q," then it would be natural for three historical biographies of one person to contain similar information, and in some cases identical wording. Their source material overlapped.[68]

Of the many possibly scenarios[69], a popular one among conservative scholars is the following: Mark was written first, based on the teachings of Peter; Matthew and Luke then wrote their narratives using Mark and Q as resources. This explains not only the similarities between the three accounts, but also helps explain why Mathew and Luke share some material in common—that is, material coming from "Q" that is not in Mark.

How do we account for the differences?[70]

In explaining their differences, the three synoptic authors probably also had independent resources or else simply selected different parts of the same sources. Obviously, they were not trying to duplicate one another.

In the case of Matthew, being one of the Twelve, he witnessed Christ's ministry firsthand.

This issue involves what scholars today call *redaction criticism*, or the study of why the authors chose to include some material and to exclude other material. It is widely recognized that each gospel writer was governed in his selection of material by his individual overriding theological purpose—in other words, his unique presentation of Christ. Matthew seems to emphasize that Jesus is the Messiah who fulfills the OT prophecies. Mark emphasizes the servanthood[71] of our Lord. Luke emphasizes that Jesus is the Son of Man, His humanness.

For the sake of completion we include John's gospel here, because John is very clear about his selection of material:

> "Therefore many other signs Jesus also performed in the presence of the disciples, which are not written in this book; but these have been written so that you may believe that Jesus is the Christ, the Son of God; and that believing you may have life in His name." (John 20:30)

Of all the events and teachings there were to choose from, John selected only a few, but he went into great detail for each. His gospel account, therefore, stands unique, set apart from the other three in its focused content and perspective. Written much later, this account was very specific and theological. He presents Christ as the Son of God, so that his readers would come to have eternal life through Him (John 20:31).

Some claim that since the gospel writers molded the source material to suit their theological ends, their history cannot be trusted. However, this conclusion is unwarranted. No historical work can include every item of historical information—selectivity is inherent to the process. And all writers of history are subject to their own interpretive framework. But there is no reason to believe that historical accuracy and theological interpretation are mutually exclusive. The gospel writers may have summarized, excerpted, and even omitted some of the stories and sayings of Jesus (in whole or in part), but that does not mean they are inaccurate.

Chapter Five

Apostolic Authority of Acts and the Letters

The Authority of the Book of Acts

The book of Acts was evidently written by the same author as The Gospel According to Luke (compare Luke 1:1-4 and Acts 1:1-3), and was therefore written by Luke, one of the companions of the apostle Paul. Clement of Alexandria (2nd century) held to Lukan authorship. Irenaeus refers to Luke as the author of the "Acts of the Apostles."[72]

The book of Acts was considered authoritative by virtue of Luke's gospel account (which was accepted) and by his association with the apostle Paul. Chronologically, its composition would have therefore followed Paul's imprisonment, so we would place it in the mid to latter part of the 1st century.

The Authority of Paul's Letters

Paul's letters (traditionally called *epistles,* which is a transliteration of the Greek word meaning "letters"[73]) are well attested, being written from AD 47-67.[74] The canonical letters associated with Paul, unlike the gospel accounts and the epistle to the Hebrews, clearly identify the author in the first line of each letter, namely Paul (the apostle). The record shows he became an eyewitness of the Lord on the day of his conversion on the road to Damascus (Acts 9; 1 Cor. 15:8).

Apostolic affirmation

It can be argued that Paul's apostleship and authority were different from that of the Twelve. He did not witness the Lord's earthly ministry, (that being the requirement for selecting a man to replace Judas as one of the Twelve, see Acts 1:21-22). Paul's witness of Jesus occurred only after Jesus' ascension. His encounter with the resurrected Christ was entirely different than that of the Twelve, theirs being a bodily, in-person witness, in contrast to Paul's seeing Jesus in a vision.[75]

Paul's apostleship is, nevertheless, well-established. The apostle Peter (assuming the authenticity of Peter's authorship of 2 Peter) wrote that Paul's letters were on the level of Scripture:

> ". . . our beloved brother Paul, according to the wisdom given him, wrote to you, as also in all his letters, speaking in them of these things, in which are some things hard to understand, which the untaught and unstable distort, as they do also *the rest of the Scriptures,* to their own destruction." (2 Peter 3:15-16, emphasis added)

Judging from the way Peter refers to "all his [Paul's] letters," we wurmise that both he and his readers were aware of a collection of Paul's letters.

Paul wrote that Peter and the other disciples accepted his apostolic authority on the level of Peter's:

> "But on the contrary, seeing that I had been entrusted with the gospel to the uncircumcised, just as Peter had been to the circumcised (for He who effectually worked for Peter in his apostleship to the circumcised effectually worked for me also to the Gentiles), and recognizing the grace that had been given to me, James and Cephas and John, who were reputed to be pillars, gave to me and Barnabas the right hand of fellowship, so that we might go to the Gentiles and they to the circumcised." (Gal. 2:7-9)

Paul claimed for himself authority directly from God as well.

> "Paul, an apostle (not sent from men nor through the agency of man, but through Jesus Christ and God the Father, who raised Him from the dead) . . . (Gal. 1:1, see also Rom. 1:5, 1 Cor. 1:1, 2 Cor. 1:1, etc.)

"For I would have you know, brethren, that the gospel which was preached by me is not according to man. For I neither received it from man, nor was I taught it, but I received it through a revelation of Jesus Christ." (Gal. 1:11-12)

The internal evidence of immediate circulation

As with the gospel accounts, some modern scholars have a penchant for challenging the obvious. Gamble, for example, sees Paul's letters as "narrowly particular in substance and purpose and make no pretense of general interest or timeless relevance" (Gamble, 36). Paul's letter to the Romans, however, was clearly written to encompass universal truths for all Christians everywhere, as is also clear from 1 Corinthians 1:1-2:

> "Paul, called as an apostle of Jesus Christ by the will of God . . . to the church of God which is at Corinth, to those who have been sanctified in Christ Jesus, saints by calling, with all who in every place call on the name of our Lord Jesus Christ, their Lord and ours." (1 Cor. 1:1-2)

Paul obviously exhibits a clear awareness of the universal impact of his teachings.

> **Some of Paul's letters have not found their way down to the present day—this is common knowledge.**

Gamble argues further that there was no reason why the churches would have desired to keep the letters that were written for a unique purpose, and that in fact some of Paul's letters have been lost to antiquity (that is, not preserved). Indeed, it is true that apparently some of Paul's letters have not found their way down to the present day (for evidence, see 1 Corinthians 5:9, 2 Corinthians 2:4)—this is common knowledge. There are, however, different constructs that fit the data as well if not better than Gamble's. It would have been natural for people to save the letters of someone as beloved as Paul was (for being the one who had evangelized them). Note the emotional departure of Paul from the Ephesian elders as seen on his third and final missionary journey:

> "When he [Paul] had said these things, he knelt down and prayed with them all. And they began to weep aloud and embraced Paul, and repeatedly kissed him, grieving especially over the word which

he had spoken, that they would not see his face again. And they were accompanying him to the ship." (Acts 20:36-38)

The most natural understanding is that the people to whom Paul ministered would have indeed wanted to preserve and circulate his writings. The Christians to whom Paul wrote would have undoubtedly seen wide value in his letters. Christians of that era, just like today, found great value in reading how the Holy Spirit dealt with specific problems in other churches—no doubt with a view to applying the principles to their own situations. Paul fostered this thinking (see 1 Corinthians 11:16). That his letters were in fact valued and circulated (in some cases immediately) can be seen in passages such as 2 Corinthians 10:10, Colossians 4:16, and 2 Peter 3:15-16.[76]

Luke makes no mention of Paul's letter-writing ministry in the book of Acts, but this is of little significance. Luke makes no mention of the gospel accounts of Matthew or Mark, either. This should not strike us as odd, for an historian must always select from a plethora of data to convey his history. Luke's concerns were more about Paul's travels and activities than about his writings. However, a correlation of the events referred to in Paul's writings with the events of the book of Acts is enlightening. Together they fill in the history of Paul's movements and activities, as well as his relationship to the churches he planted. And such cross referencing lends credence to the historicity of both sets of writings.

Later testimony about Paul's authority

In AD 96, Clement of Rome clearly had access to some of Paul's letters.[77] From the early 2nd century, most of Paul's letters (with the exception of the Pastorals of 1 and 2 Timothy and Titus) circulated as a collection.[78]

Some scholars scoff at genuine authorship of some of the canonical Pauline writings, for example the Pastoral letters, Ephesians, and Colossians. However, for the author of those books that are attributed to Paul to lace his writings with a deep piety and a call to ethical and spiritual living would be incongruous with knowingly deceiving his readers about his identity. To be sure, pseudonymous writing in general was common in the 2nd century, but there is no evidence that the canonical Pauline writings were authored by anyone other than the apostle Paul.

"Despite the consistent evidence from the early Church outside the New Testament, many scholars assert, in the most confident terms, that writing letters in the name of another was common practice. Nowhere is evidence cited that any member of a New Testament Church accepted the idea that a pious believer could write something in the name of an apostle and expect the writing to be welcomed."[79]

We do not know for sure who collected Paul's writings; some suggest Luke, and others, Timothy. Either would be a natural candidate for this honor as both were close companions of Paul's through much of his ministry—but the final determination must be left unresolved.

We do not know when the Pastorals (1 and 2 Timothy and Titus) were included in the earlier collection of Paul's writings, but this happened prior to the time of the Muratorian Canon (late 2nd century),[80] which referenced them.

New Testament historian F. F. Bruce states: "There are relatively few variant readings in the textual tradition of Paul's letters . . ."[81] Apparently, a single codex[82] into which they originally were compiled became the master-copy for subsequent manuscripts.

THE AUTHORITY OF THE GENERAL LETTERS

The General Epistles took longer to be accepted by the church as authoritative. This is probably because of the relative late date of writing (except, possibly, for James). Therefore, these epistles did not attain wide circulation as early as the four gospels and Paul's letters. However the early church accepted the genuine authorship of each of these as being apostolic, and therefore authoritative.

James

The identity of the author is stated at the beginning of the letter, but the question arises about *which* James it was. Lacking no further clarification to the readers, the author must have been an individual well-known to the intended audience (and to the immediately subsequent generations of Christians). Of the two most prominent men named James in the early church, the apostle James was one, and he was martyred (see Acts 12) at a time much earlier than the book of James was most likely written. The other well-known James is the half-brother of Jesus that Paul refers to in Galatians 1:19 and who was prominent in the Jerusalem church (see Acts 15). Because of his clear association with the Twelve and his obvious standing among the apostles and elders at Jerusalem, conservative scholars believe this James to have authored this letter. It was thus considered authoritative.[83]

> The book of James has had a long history of debate because of its supposed tension with the teaching of Paul.

The book of James was certainly quoted in 1 Clement and the Shepherd of Hermas (mid-2nd century),[84] so its existence was attested to early on. Eusebius accepted it as canonical in the 4th century.

Many have pointed out that the book of James has had a long history of debate (even to the time of Luther) because of its supposed tension with the teaching of Paul. However, the fact that someone like Luther would question it presupposes the virtually unanimous assumption of the book's canonical status![85] James did in fact come to be recognized as canonical in all parts of the ancient church, despite the fact that some hesitated. No one (among the orthodox) rejected the book.

The date for this book has been placed as early as the first part of the AD 40s to no later than AD 62 (when James died).

Peter

Two letters are identified internally as being authored by Peter. The overwhelming early church testimony is that this is the well-known apostle Peter, at least in the case of the first letter. Polycarp (writing in AD 135) was acquainted with the book of 1 Peter, as was Irenaeus (toward the end of the 2nd century).

> Second Peter is probably the most disputed of all the canonical books, both in ancient times and modern.

Eusebius identified it being "undisputed," as he himself accepted it. Present-day objections to 1 Peter's genuine authorship are based primarily on internal evidence and go against the overwhelming testimony of the early church. The date of Peter's first letter was probably AD 62-63.

The book of 2 Peter is apparently the author's second letter ("This is now, beloved, the second letter I am writing to you . . ." 2 Peter 3:1). The author claims to be a personal witness of the Lord (2 Peter 1:16-18), so it is most natural to view the two letters as being authored by the same individual, Peter.

Second Peter is probably the most disputed of all the canonical books, both in ancient times and modern, the main objection being the assumed "pseudonymous" authorship of the book, namely that someone used Peter's name to give weight to their letter. It has been suggested that, since there were so many forgeries in Peter's name, the early church moved very carefully in separating out 2 Peter from the other books. Eusebius accepted it as canonical in the 4th century and it has been accepted ever since. The date of writing for 2 Peter was probably just before his death in AD 65 (see 2 Peter 1:13-14).

John

Three canonical letters are attributed to the apostle John. Allusions to these occur in many of the earliest church writers. The first clear reference to a specific letter from John is found in Papias's writings in mid-2nd century. Irenaeus refers to 1 and 2 John explicitly as being written by John the disciple of Jesus. The second and third letters are not as well attested, but this could be due to their diminutive length and the fact that they do not contain such well-focused teaching as do other letters; clearly, therefore, these writings would be less quoted. Never did any early church writer attribute the authorship of these letters to anyone other than the apostle John.[86]

Many present-day scholars, however, assert there was a Johannine school of followers of the apostle who formulated these writings and attributed them to John, but the existence of such a "school" is far from proved. The evidence weighs clearly in favor of the apostle John's authorship.[87]

The date of writing of these three letters has been suggested as early as AD 80-85 to the early 90s.

Jude

The book of Jude was questioned for awhile because of the author's reference to a "book of Enoch" (Jude 1:14). Jude refers to himself as the brother of James and was presumably therefore the half-brother of Jesus—and on this weight the book was eventually accepted. The Muratorian Canon (late 2nd century[88]) includes this letter, and Tertullian and Clement of Alexandria considered it to be canonical. Eusebius identified it as a disputed letter but listed it as canonical.

One of the main objections to Jude's authorship is that the Greek language used in the book is not in keeping for a Galilean Jew of humble upbringing. However, history is replete with examples of people rising above their lowly backgrounds. For a more recent example, Fredrick Douglas of 19th century America was born and raised as a slave, escaped to the north at age twenty, and went on to become an eloquent orator, even running as a vice-presidential candidate for the United States. Thus it is not unreasonable to believe someone like Jude could rise above his humble background. The date of its writing was probably the mid-60s.

THE AUTHORITY OF THE BOOK OF REVELATION

The book of Revelation came to acceptance later than most other NT books, due undoubtedly to its relatively late date of composition (last decade of the 1st century). It was almost universally accepted during the 2nd century, however.[89] One of many 2nd century testimonies is Justin Martyr's reference to Revelation as having been written by John the apostle. Irenaeus quotes from it extensively. The evidence is so strong for John's authorship that some have said it is the most well-attested of all NT books.[90] Since its authorship was accepted as being that of John, the book of the Revelation was therefore accepted as authoritative.

There was a short period of time when the book came under question due to the Montanist's heavy reliance on it for their theological aberrations. Some felt that if the Montanists emphasized that particular book, maybe it was suspect. However, in time its place of authority came to be uncontested.[91]

The date of composition was probably AD 95-96.

THE AUTHORITY OF THE LETTER TO THE HEBREWS

The antiquity of the letter to the Hebrews is established by the extensive quotations in 1 Clement (AD 90-110). The early church used it widely, although it presented a problem because of the question of authorship. The earliest collections of Paul's writings included this letter, and it was placed along with Paul's letters right after the book of Romans. Thus it was assumed to be Pauline in authorship. Clement of Alexandria (late 2nd – early 3rd century) and Origen (early 3rd century) believed that Paul wrote the letter.

Others, however, like Irenaeus and the Muratorian Canon, "agree that Paul was not the author."[92] Irenaeus thought Barnabas was the author.

Tertullian (AD 196-212) cites Barnabas as the author of Hebrews, "a man sufficiently accredited by God, as being one whom Paul had stationed next to himself."[93]

Astute students of the Word will recognize that many typical Pauline characteristics are absent from the book, for example: opening identification of himself as its author, the standard "grace and peace" salutation, and the doctrine of justification. These observations are countered with various theories:

> Because he was the apostle to the Gentiles, Paul wrote it anonymously and in the Hebrew language and Luke (or someone else close to Paul) translated it into Greek. This would account for the differences in style from Paul's usual writings. Indeed, some think Paul originally delivered this as a sermon in Hebrew, and someone transcribed it into Greek.

> Paul, being the apostle to the Gentiles, wanted to assume a more modest approach to a book aimed at Jewish Christians. Paneaenus (AD 180-192) wrote:

> "Since the Lord, being the apostle of the Almighty, was sent to the Hebrews, Paul, having been sent to the Gentiles, through modesty did not inscribe himself as an apostle of the Hebrews, both because of respect for the Lord and because he wrote to the Hebrews also out of his abundance, being a preacher and apostle for the Gentiles."[94]

The authorship of Hebrews has been debated to this very day. We must conclude that we simply do not know for sure who its author was.

> The subject matter of the book (the supremacy of Christ over the Levitical sacrificial system) required a different style of writing.

The authorship has been debated to this very day with various other suggestions being been made, but none has commanded universal appeal.[95] Today, very few defend the idea that Paul wrote Hebrews. We must conclude that we simply do not know for sure who its author was. As a result, the question of authorship has a somewhat troublesome history. However, the early church eventually came to accept Hebrews as authoritative based on its universal usage, its internal character being consonant with "the faith," and its exalted view of Christ.

Dates for composition range from AD 60 to 100. However a date earlier than AD 70 would explain the absence of any reference to the destruction of the temple which would have otherwise provided significant support to the author's theme of Christ replacing the OT sacrificial system.

Chapter Six

Influencing the Spread

Before we look at later church fathers and their role in identifying the NT Canon, we need to look at the movements and development that provided the background to their writings. We can identify four specific forces that probably encouraged the spread of the documents which we now call the New Testament:

1) The apostolic nature of the "received" writings.
2) The rise of "variant" teachings.[96]
3) Increased persecution.
4) The development of new book-making technology.

Apostolic Roots of the Writings

Early transmission of apostolic teaching

Natural desire. All evidence we have points to the fact that early Christians believed they were following the Person and teachings of Jesus Christ. Yet there is no evidence at all that Jesus, the object of their devotion and faith, left any personally written teachings or memoirs. Somehow, from an historical perspective, an indelible, incredible impression was left on them concerning the reality and importance of the Lord Jesus Christ. The apostles were the link. There is no other sufficient explanation for the widespread and early belief in Christ than that the apostles were revolutionized by their relationship with Jesus of Nazareth, who they came to believe was

God in the flesh, the Messiah. They were apparently convinced of the need to spread the teachings of their Master widely, and their enthusiasm and devotion spread quickly. The insatiable thirst for the apostles' teachings is evident from the earliest of times. At the beginning of the 2nd century, although the apostles had all passed away the historical record gives strong evidence that their teachings lived on unabated. Their influence on the early church was huge! There was, therefore, a natural desire for the early church to learn all they could from the apostolic teaching.

> The early Christians believed they were following the Person and teachings of Jesus Christ.

Oral traditions. Fortunate was the person who had personal access to an apostle for a firsthand account or the person who had memories of firsthand exposure to an apostle's teachings. Subsequent generations had the teachings as they were passed down orally. The term *oral tradition* is used to describe apostolic teachings that were circulated by word-of-mouth.[97] In particular, many relied on the "sayings of Christ" that were rehearsed orally and circulated from church to church by traveling Christians. Since Christians didn't have these things in written form initially, there was a strong reliance on memorization.

Written documents. As the apostles began to write their accounts of Christ's life and ministry as well as their epistles, copies were made and circulated (as we have already noted above).

Widespread use of apostolic writings

Very early in the historical record we see evidence of widespread use of the apostolic writings, probably due to the fact that the original witnesses were no longer available. Carson and Moo write,

> "The Gospels, Acts, the thirteen Paulines, 1 Peter, and 1 John are universally accepted very early; most of the remaining contours of the New Testament canon are already established by the time of Eusebius [early 4th century]."[98]

SPREAD OF "VARIANT" TEACHING

In time, given the spread of Christianity, doctrinal differences arose. New gospels and writings began to circulate, claiming authority for doctrinal variants. The need became increasingly clear to identify and defend the genuine writings imbued with apostolic authority and to recognize and reject those lacking such authority. Some today assert that the rise of these "movements" was within the mainstream of Christianity, reflecting a diversity and pluralism in the early church. However, this is simply not the case, as these movements were resisted from the earliest signs of their rising influence. They were never seen as mainstream to say the least, nor were they tolerated.

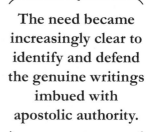

The need became increasingly clear to identify and defend the genuine writings imbued with apostolic authority.

Judaizers in the 1st century

While much of the apostolic writings provided positive teaching about Jesus Christ and Christian living, there was a significant amount expressly written to oppose or correct false teachings that rose up against the apostles' teachings. For example, the book of Galatians addressed what some today call "Judaizers," those who wanted to make obedience to the law of Moses required for all Christians. In particular, they emphasized circumcision for Gentiles as necessary for salvation. Paul saw this as a significant threat to the gospel of grace and wrote passionately to the Galatian church about it:

> "I am amazed that you are so quickly deserting Him who called you by the grace of Christ, for a different gospel; which is really not another; only there are some who are disturbing you and want to distort the gospel of Christ. But even if we, or an angel from heaven, should preach to you a gospel contrary to what we have preached to you, he is to be accursed! As we have said before, so I say again now, if any man is preaching to you a gospel contrary to what you received, he is to be accursed!" (Gal. 1:6-9)

Paul predicted, when meeting with the Ephesian church elders, that false teachers would continue to rise up:

> "I know that after my departure savage wolves will come in among you, not sparing the flock; and from among your own selves men will arise, speaking perverse things, to draw away the disciples after them." (Acts 20:29-30)

Writings claiming apostolic authority began to surface which taught different doctrine than that of the apostles.

> ". . . [we ask] that you not be quickly shaken from your composure or be disturbed either by a spirit or a message or a letter as if from us, to the effect that the day of the Lord has come." (2 Thess. 2:2)

False teachers and cult leaders wrote and fostered their own "scriptures" to counter what was handed down from the apostles (whether orally or in writing). Some of them justified their "new" writings from the comments made in The Gospel According to John:

> "Therefore many other signs Jesus also performed in the presence of the disciples, which are not written in this book; but these have been written so that you may believe that Jesus is the Christ, the Son of God; and that believing you may have life in His name." (John 20:30-31, see also 21:25)

They claimed they were just providing some of the missing details that John and the others had left out. Over time, therefore, the need arose in the face of Judaizers for identifying those documents which were genuinely apostolic and for rejecting those that were not.

Gnostics during the 2nd – 5th centuries

> **Gnosticism was considered the greatest threat to the church of the early centuries.**

Gnosticism's beginning was gradual, and it flourished alongside Christianity for three centuries. One of its more well-known proponents was Valentinus, who broke away from the church[99] and established a school to spread his doctrine (AD 140-165). This teaching was considered the greatest threat to the church of the early centuries.

The teachings of Gnosticism were, until recently, known only through the writings of the church fathers as they defended the true faith against it. Admittedly the best source of information is usually not from the opponents of a viewpoint. However, in 1945 at Nag Hammadi in Egypt, a collection of manuscripts was discovered which dates to about AD 400. This discovery included many Gnostic writings and corroborated much of what we already knew through the church fathers. In fact, many conservative NT scholars point out that little was added to our understanding of this movement that was not already known, despite the sensationalism of gnostic sympathizers today.

Basic tenets of Gnosticism. There were many varieties and shades of Gnosticism, but a few central concepts surface. The term comes from the Greek word *gnosis*, which means "knowledge." Gnostic thinking saw people as souls temporarily imprisoned in physical bodies; their only escape is through a special *gnosis*, or knowledge, about their origin and their destiny. The goal is to return to the realm of the Highest Ideal or Absolute Truth.

The Creator God of the Bible, in gnostic thinking, was not the ultimate god of the entire universe. The absolute and ultimate god of all is perfectly pure and holy; he (or it) is absolute wisdom and truth. From this ultimate god emanated a series of beings (or eons) out of whom flowed other emanations. The further an emanation was from the ultimate god, the less holy, pure, and wise it was—and the more physical and material it became. At some point, one of those emanations, called by some the Demiurge, became the Creator God of the OT. As Gnostics believed, the original, ultimate god was too good, too holy, and too pure to create a physical universe (see illustration below). But the Demiurge was sufficiently digressed from the 'Absolute Truth' that creation of material substance was possible. As one author puts it, the Gnostics believed that "the one whom most Christians naively worship as creator, God, and Father is, in reality, only the image of the true God."[100]

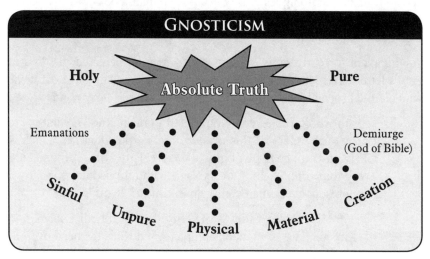

Figure 3. A Gnostic View of God

The goal for humans, therefore, was to seek *gnosis* or special knowledge in order to transcend this physical (unholy) earthly existence and ultimately to arrive back at union with the ultimate Truth.

The Gnostics developed their own set of writings that mixed this neo-platonic belief with Christian concepts and words. They had a particular attraction to the writings of the apostle John because of his use of Greek concepts like light, life, knowledge, and, especially the "Logos" of John chapter 1. These words and concepts lent themselves to being expropriated by the Gnostics and used to support their teachings.

Implications. Gnostic teaching carried significant implications for the orthodox teaching of the incarnation of the Son of God in the Person of Jesus Christ, in particular what theologians call the *hypostatic union*[101]—the teaching that Christ was truly God *and* truly man. If Christ were truly God, according to Gnostic teaching He would be too pure and holy to inhabit a physical body. If, on the other hand, Christ were truly human (i.e. physical man), He could not be God because He would be too sinful, too far from the absolute Truth. Either Christ was divine or He was human, but not both, they said.

This thinking was contrary to the clear presentation of the accepted apostolic texts describing Jesus as *both* God *and* man. The Gnostics rejected those portions of the apostolic writings that affirmed Jesus' incarnation, God becoming a man.

Incipient (or early hints of) Gnosticism can be detected in some of Paul's letters. His letter to the Colossians, with his polemic against those who claimed special insight apart from Jesus Christ, is very pointed:

> ". . . to whom [believers] God willed to make known what is the riches of the glory of this mystery among the Gentiles, which is Christ in you, the hope of glory. We proclaim Him, admonishing every man and teaching every man with all wisdom, so that we may present every man complete in Christ." (Col. 1:27-28)

> "For in Him all the fullness of Deity dwells in bodily form, and in Him you have been made complete, and He is the head over all rule and authority." (Col. 2:9-10)

In short, there is no need for further enlightenment or insight apart from Christ. In him, all mystery is revealed.

The church's response. The church began to question The Gospel According to John because of the use Gnostics made of it, but eventually that gospel account was fully embraced like the other three.

Supporters and sympathizers of Gnosticism today sometimes speak of a conspiracy in which the early church became politically motivated and thus covered up "the truth." However, the evidence is abundant that Gnostic writings arose long after the apostolic writings and did conflict with them. Thus Gnostic teachings were rejected on solid historical grounds. The early church was not "insecure," nor did the Christians of that time have ulterior motives in destroying Gnostic documents, as some have suggested. In fact, the debates were *not* expunged from church writings. The early believers simply had no interest in preserving writings which were clearly erroneous, and they certainly did not hold on to them to satisfy the "intellectual" curiosity of the academics of later centuries! Their concern was for truth! As "orthodox"[102] Christianity gained in prominence, the writings of the Gnostics fell into obscurity.

Marcionites in the 2nd century

Marcion of Sinope (in present-day Turkey) was born in AD 100 and became a wealthy Christian ship owner. He wrote only one literary work, which has been lost. What we know about him is gleaned from what was written against him. Others wrote with Marcion's influence, and thus the movement became large (though not as large as the Gnostics). Marcion himself was probably influenced by early Gnostic thought.

> Marcion was the first (that we know of) to publish a fixed collection of books that he considered authoritative.

He was the first (that we know of) to publish a fixed collection of books that he considered authoritative (latter part of the 2nd century).[103] This has been called the Marcion Canon. This list excluded the OT and anything that in his view implied the legitimacy of the Mosaic law. He included Luke and ten of Paul's letters (but not the Pastorals—1 and 2 Timothy and Titus).

His teachings. Marcion struggled with the question of why a God who is almighty—all-powerful—would create a world that includes suffering, pain, and disease. He rejected the OT and considered the God of the OT as cruel and inferior to the God of all goodness. Marcion regarded matter as evil and therefore held to a docetic view of the incarnation—that is, Christ only *seemed* to have a body, but in reality did not. It follows that he denied the resurrection of the body as well as advocating a strict ascetic lifestyle.

Marcion directly challenged apostolic teaching because he thought that the twelve apostles misunderstood Jesus, wrongly believing Him to be the Messiah of the Jews. However, he was devoted passionately to Paul, believing him to be the only apostle to faithfully preserve the teaching of Jesus in its purity. He also held Luke's gospel account to be authoritative (possibly because of Luke's association with Paul). In his view, the apostles corrupted the teachings of Jesus with legalism. Even in Luke's account, Marcion purged things which were inconsistent with his (Marcion's) understanding of truth. Luke's references to the OT were removed because they smacked of legalism to him. He also eliminated references to John the Baptist due to John's pivotal role between the old and new covenants. He removed the birth of Christ as it was connected clearly to OT genealogy. Jesus, he believed, simply appeared supernaturally.

Marcion even removed those parts of Paul's writings which he judged were in error (for example Galatians 3:16–4:6, because of its reference to Abraham). Other changes were made as well, justifying them as corrections to apostolic errors or copyist interpolations. All his changes can be explained on the basis of his beliefs. Interestingly, because Marcion taught celibacy, membership in his "new church" was maintained only by conversions.

Implications. The apostolic witness of the twelve original disciples was nullified in Marcion's teachings. He failed to see Christ as the fulfillment of God's plan of salvation through the OT. He also failed to recognize the "right hand of fellowship" about which Paul himself spoke concerning his relationship to the other apostles (Gal. 2:9).

The church's response. Some see in Marcion and his movement (which became quite widespread and lasted about a century) the suggestion that the authoritative texts in Christianity had not yet been generally accepted; orthodox theology had yet to be settled. However, that presupposes there was little recognition of what was truly apostolic before Marcion. Rather, the overwhelming denunciation of Marcion and the defense by the majority of the churches and church leaders speaks to the general acceptance of the recognized texts and theology among the early Christians. In other words, if Marcion was reacting and rejecting, then there must have been something well established to react *to* and to reject. We have argued elsewhere in this book that there was much agreement until the "false" teachings became more invasive among the churches. Metzger puts it this way:

> "It was in opposition to Marcion's criticism that the church first became fully conscious of its inheritance of apostolic writings. As Grant aptly puts it, 'Marcion forced more orthodox Christians to examine their own presuppositions and to state more clearly what they already believed.'"[104]

In the end, the church rejected Marcion's teaching as being contrary to the "received" apostolic writings and oral traditions.

Montanists of the 2nd – 3rd centuries

Montanism as a movement dated from the second half of the 2nd century. The name derives from its founder, Montanus. It was a kind of 2nd century extreme charismatic movement, marked by ecstatic outbursts and tongues. Its spread through the church was swift.

What they believed. Montanus taught that *he* was the inspired instrument of a new outpouring of the Spirit. He and his followers developed ascetic traits and rigors in the face of growing worldliness in the church. Some consider this a reaction to the clerical aristocracy that had arisen in the church, which had become more and more institutionalized.[105] Women were accepted into leadership. In fact, two women were closely associated with Montanus, prophetesses named Prisca and Maximilla, who left their husbands to follow him. Adherents of Montanism gathered their own writings like sacred documents, many of which were apocalyptic. Montanists expected the imminent end of the world.

> The conflict with Montanists led to an increasing movement to identify all the truly authoritative texts.

The church's response. While there is some truth to the fact that worldliness had crept into the church, the early believers nonetheless maintained that the writings of Montanists did not reflect the accepted apostolic writings. Interestingly, the book of Revelation became suspect because the Montanists relied on it, but eventually the faithful accepted it as authoritative. Again, the conflict with Montanists led to an increasing movement to identify all the truly authoritative texts.

PERSECUTION BY ROME AGAINST CHRISTIANS

In the early days of Christianity, the Roman government saw this new movement as subversive and a threat to Roman culture and thinking. With increasing persecution, the government pressured Christians to surrender the writings that were evidently fueling their passion and allegiance. The punishment for resisting such imperial efforts included imprisonment, torture, and in some cases, death. It became a matter of conscience as to which writings the Christians were willing to suffer or die for. Undoubtedly, those books considered authoritative were guarded well, but lesser books not having the same authority were more readily surrendered. Thus, for example, the so-called Gospel of Thomas was more likely to be relinquished in the face of persecution than, say, Matthew's gospel. Providentially, persecution effected a kind of "natural selection." The authoritative books, the ones held in high regard, were more likely to survive than other writings.

> It became a matter of conscience as to which writings the Christians were willing to suffer and die for.

BOOK-MAKING TECHNOLOGY

Scrolls – "the old way"

Prior to the 2nd century, almost all writing in the ancient Near East was rendered on scrolls usually made from the papyrus plant. Scrolls were limited to about thirty-five feet in length (about the length needed for The Gospel According to Luke or the book of Acts). Beyond this length a scroll would be too unwieldly. This limited the number of writings that could be kept together on one scroll. Collecting and transporting scrolls was done with a box or container and would obviously have been cumbersome. Individual Christians did not have pocket Bibles, to be sure!

Codex or "leaf-book" – "the new way"

By the end of the 1st century and beginning of the second, a new technology for writing had emerged: the codex, or leaf-book. Initially, the leaves were made from papyri, but vellum fashioned from animal skins came into more prominent use because it was more durable.

In codex form, many books or writings could be assembled in one volume, enhancing the portability of the writings. This resulted in the association of various writings together. In fact, by the beginning of the 2nd century, Paul's writings were circulating as a group, probably facilitated by the more convenient form of the codex. The net result was that the rise of codex technology increased the grouping and circulation of the apostolic writings among the churches.

CONCLUSION

We have seen that four forces influenced the identification of the accepted, authoritative texts that became the NT. Each asserted influence, the sum of which is noteworthy, even, one could say, "providential."

Chapter Seven

The Apostolic Fathers

The term *apostolic fathers* refers to certain writers who followed very shortly after (in some cases were contemporary with) the time of the apostles, spanning roughly AD 95-150. (The same term is conventionally used of their writings, with the initial letters capitalized, i.e. the Apostolic Fathers.) While we have seen in previous chapters a sampling of what they wrote, we will now look at them a little closer. These writers seldom made direct quotations from NT writings but clearly exhibited knowledge of them; they included many allusions to, or borrowed phrases from, NT writings.

From the apostolic fathers we learn much about the spread and acceptance of the apostles' writings.

Clement of Rome – Epistle to the Corinthians (ca. AD 95-96)[106]

While the document attributed to Clement of Rome is apparently anonymous, it has been associated from the earliest times with the church leader of Rome who was "active in that city during the closing decades of the 1st century AD"[107] Many believe this to be the Clement referred to by Paul in Philippians 4:3. In his letter, Clement addressed younger leaders in Corinth who rose up against the elders of the church, calling them (that is, the younger leaders) to repentance. He quoted extensively from the OT and also loosely quoted from the Lord (from Matthew or Luke's gospels). It is not certain, however, if he was quoting from memory or which gospel account he was referencing, or, for that matter, whether he was quoting from written texts or from oral tradition. Clement refered to letters written by Paul, specifically citing the ones to the Corinthians and alluding to the letters to churches in Rome, Galatia, Philippi and Ephesus. He was also evidently well acquainted with the epistle to the Hebrews.

However, "If Clement evidences the powerful influence of the writings later incorporated into the New Testament, he still has no formal theory of a New Testament Scripture or canon. While the tradition that derives from Jesus and His apostles is authoritative, it is not authoritative in a specific form; at this period, no distinction is made between oral and written tradition."[108]

IGNATIUS OF ANTIOCH – SEVEN LETTERS (CA. AD 110)

Ignatius was the second or third "bishop" of Antioch in Syria.[109] He wrote seven letters on the way to his martyrdom in Rome. His primary source for authority was the apostolic preaching about the life, death, and resurrection of Jesus Christ:

> "As for me, the archives [i.e. authoritative writings] are Jesus Christ; the unadulterated archives are His cross and His death and His resurrection, and the faith which is through him—In these I wish to be justified through your prayers."[110]

Ignatius knew of Paul's letters (specifically 1 Corinthians, Ephesians, Romans, Galatians, Philippians, Colossians and 1 Thessalonians), Matthew, John, and possibly Luke.

THE DIDACHE (FIRST HALF OF THE 2ND CENTURY)

Written by an unknown author, the Didache is a short manual of moral instruction and church practice. It refers to itinerant apostles and prophets, but their authority was declining at the time of writing, subject more and more to precautions that all teaching had to rest "ultimately on the authority of the traditional teaching deriving from the Lord."[111] The book quotes twice from the OT and refers to words of Jesus from the Matthew's gospel. The author was possibly acquainted with Paul's first letter to the Corinthians based on some similarities of words, phrases, and structure.

Papias of Hierapolis "Exposition of the Sayings of the Lord" (AD 70 to ca. 140)

The church in Hierapolis was established by Epaphras, a co-missionary of Paul's (Col. 4:12-13). It is thought that Papias, bishop of the church in Hierapolis, had heard the apostle John preach; some even think Papias was a disciple of John.[112] He was a friend of Polycarp of Smyrna (see below).

Only fragmentary copies of his writing exist today. He was the first of the apostolic fathers to take a specific interest in the earlier Christian writings. He was eager to learn as much as he could from the apostles, as relayed to him through others:

> **Papias was the first of the apostolic fathers to take a specific interest in the early Christian writings.**

> "If ever anyone came who had been a follower of the presbyters I inquired into the words of the presbyters, what Andrew or Peter or Philip or Thomas or James or John or Matthew or any other of the Lord's disciples had said, and what Aristion and the presbyter John the Lord's disciples, were saying. For I did not think that information from books would help me so much as the utterances of the living and surviving voice."[113]

He apparently knew the daughters of Philip (mentioned in Acts 21:8) and clearly indicated that Mark recorded the life and teachings of Jesus as told by Peter:

> "The presbyter used to say this: Mark, having become Peter's interpreter (or spokesman or secretary) wrote down accurately all that he remembered [of Peter's preaching] without, however, recording in order the things said or done by the Lord.... For he was careful of one thing—to omit nothing of what he had heard or to falsify anything in them."[114]

Papias apparently also knew of John's gospel, 1 Peter, 1 John, and Revelation, but made no specific references to Paul's writings.

The Epistle of Barnabas (Possibly AD 130)

We know nothing about the author. Some later church fathers thought this was the Barnabas associated with Paul. Others felt this could not have been, because the writer refered to the fall of Jerusalem (AD 70) as having already taken place, thus placing him at too late a date to be Paul's associate.

Written very much as a theological tract, it was concerned to prove that the death of Christ on the cross was a sacrifice that fulfilled a plan set forth in the OT. Though radically anti-Jewish, he quoted both frequently and fairly accurately from the OT. In fact, the writer was very much a scholarly author who had read widely and quoted frequently from various sources.

He was acquainted with Matthew's gospel and seems to echo portions from 1 and 2 Timothy.

POLYCARP OF SMYRNA (BETWEEN AD 110 AND 135)

Polycarp was a church leader in Smyrna and a friend of Papias. His writings are closely related to those of Ignatius. Making about a dozen references to the OT, he also showed wide acquaintance with the NT, especially Matthew and Luke, but also Romans, 1 Corinthians, Galatians, Ephesians, Philippians, 2 Thessalonians, 1 and 2 Timothy, Hebrews, 1 John, and 1 Peter. This is the most for any of the apostolic fathers.

THE SHEPHERD OF HERMAS[115]

This anonymous work was written sometime around the end of the 1st century or beginning of the 2nd century (but could be as late as mid-2nd century). The book was comprised of a religious allegory featuring a rugged individual dressed like a shepherd as Hermas's guide. It reflects a similar literary genre as "Pilgrim's Progress" by John Bunyan (1678). The book includes very few if any quotations from any literature, let alone OT or NT, though it possibly makes some allusions to Matthew, Ephesians, and James.

> The Shepherd of Hermas was one of the most popular books among early Christians and was widely copied.

The Shepherd of Hermas was one of the most popular books among early Christians and was widely copied. For a long time it was considered inspired. Although some claim it was "acknowledged without reservation as scripture" by Irenaeus, Clement of Alexandria, and Tertullian, this is saying too much. While these writers may have quoted from the Shepherd of Hermas, and, in at least the case of Clement of Alexandria referred to parts of it as revelation, this does not automatically mean the book was accepted as canonical.[116] In Irenaeus's case, the Shepherd of Hermas was rejected because it was not recognized in the churches in earlier times.[117]

In time, however, the church finally rejected the Shepherd of Hermas as not being authoritative. The noted scholar Carl F. H. Henry, in discussing the history of the word "canon," writes, "The actual term canon apparently did not come into regular use in connection with the Bible until the middle of the fourth century, when Athanasius describes The Shepherd of Hermas as 'not belonging to the canon.' Yet the idea of such a list of authoritative books which were read in the Church's public worship services, in contradistinction from other books however edifying, is older."[118]

THE "SO-CALLED" SECOND EPISTLE OF CLEMENT (AD 120-170)

This is clearly a transcript of an early Christian sermon, once thought to be a second letter of Clement of Rome. Scholars now feel this is not the case, although a replacement attribution has not been agreed upon. The purpose of the epistle was to inculcate personal holiness. There are quotes from the OT, and the author was apparently acquainted with Matthew, Luke, 1 Corinthians, and Ephesians. He may have known Hebrews, James and 1 Peter, judging from internal similarities. Of the eleven times he cites the words of Jesus, only six are found in the canonical gospels.

CONCLUSION

The value of the Apostolic Fathers (that is, their writings) is found in their attestation to an early date for most of the NT writings. These provide the literary/historical link between the teachings and authority of the apostolic writers and subsequent generations of Christ-followers.

Chapter Eight

The Later Church Fathers

By the end of the apostolic period, the four gospels were regarded as a closed collection and accepted throughout the whole church.[119] Most of Paul's writings, Acts, and Revelation were accepted as authoritative by the end of the 1st century.[120] The rest (Hebrews, James, 1 and 2 Peter, 1, 2, and 3 John and Jude) were not recognized by all at first, but eventually were accepted as authoritative. A few other writings were debated—for example, the Shepherd of Hermas—but were eventually rejected.

The local churches of the early post-apostolic times were not associated in a denominational sense with a headquarters or central governing body. To be sure, the general movement was away from the biblical pattern of localized leadership by elders. However the primacy of Rome in the Roman Catholic tradition emerged slowly and much later, and was not a factor in the recognizing of authoritative writings. In the beginning the church leaders in Rome were simply a few of the many voices who addressed the identification of authoritative writings. Put simply, Christ did not leave any one ecclesiastical or theological center that could "authorize" the definitive list of Canon writings.[121] As a result, each local church determined for itself which writings were to be considered authentic and used for worship and life.

Geographical tendencies

Churches in the same geographical regions began to influence one another. Strong personalities or gifted people arose who carried increasing sway on theological matters. This led to the rise of bishops who began to have controlling authority over churches in a region. In an era before modern communication technology, these influences were initially somewhat localized, leading to regional differences in perspectives. This in turn affected the different regions' views of what was authoritative. These theological tendencies eventually became most apparent in the variations between churches in the West (Europe) and churches in the East (Egypt, Turkey, Syria, etc.). Yet what was remarkable was the substantial unity among almost all churches regarding the authoritative writings that became canonical.

> What was remarkable was the substantial unity among almost all churches regarding the authoritative writings that became canonical.

CRITERIA USED BY THE CHURCHES FOR INCLUSION INTO THE CANON

Three criteria for recognizing whether a writing was authoritative came to be accepted broadly in the 2nd century.[122]

Apostolic authority

Was it written by an apostle or an immediate associate of an apostle? The early Christians believed that if a writing was apostolic, it was, by virtue of that fact, authoritative. Therefore, writings that were clearly authored by an apostle were accepted. Writings of, for example, Mark, who was closely associated with Peter, were also accepted because of Peter's authority. The same could be said of Luke (who was associated closely with Paul). In the case of Paul's writings and the Synoptic Gospels, this first criterion was sufficient since they had been accepted as authentically apostolic and therefore authoritative from the earliest records.

The Shepherd of Hermas is an example of a work that was written much too late to be apostolic. Also, the church rejected anything that was pseudonymous, that is, falsely attributed to an apostle (see 2 Thessalonians 2:2 and 3:17 for a NT example of this rejection). Carson and Moo assert:

> "That pseudonymous apocalypses were widespread is demonstrable; that pseudonymous letters were widespread is entirely unsupported

by the evidence; that *any* pseudonymity was knowingly accepted into the New Testament cannon is denied by the evidence. . . . This leaves very little space for the common modern assertion that pseudonymity was a widely acceptable practice in the ancient church."[123]

Acceptance and usage by the churches

Did a particular writing find general and broad acceptance among the churches during the time the Canon was being recognized? Was a writing being treated alongside Jewish Scriptures? Since all literature of antiquity was copied by hand (the moveable type printing press was not invented until the mid 15th century), there were relatively few manuscript copies of the apostolic writings. As a result, church services were composed heavily of public reading from the OT Scriptures and from apostolic writings. This criterion for canonical status assumed that a book which enjoyed wide acceptance over a long period of time was more likely to be considered authoritative than one accepted in a limited region or for a limited time span.[124] In other words, the consensus of the churches as a whole was important.

> A book which enjoyed wide acceptance over a long period of time was more likely to be considered authoritative than one accepted for a limited time span.

The book of Hebrews, despite debates over authorship among the church fathers, was accepted on the basis of its universal usage. It should be noted that the early church did not see Hebrews as pseudonymous, but rather anonymous (the author did not identify himself within the book). Further, the early church believed the book was written at a sufficiently early date so as to be considered apostolic. In fact, it circulated with Paul's epistles early in the 2nd century.

Recent research into the quotations contained in the early church writers from various sources has shown that "there is a sharp demarcation in actual frequency of usage between the New Testament books and all other claimants; actual usage was establishing the canon."[125] In other words, historically, the actual use of the twenty-seven books known today as the NT was widespread in the 2nd century.

Affirmed Spiritual Validation

Did a writing conform to what was called the "rule of faith"? That is, did it measure up to what had already been accepted as normative by the church? This rule of faith was "a summary of the tenets held in common by the churches of apostolic foundation: it is closely related to what is called 'apostolic tradition.'"[126]

Contrary to some modern scholars, the early Christians were aware of the need to distinguish between that which was "orthodox" and that which was "heretical"; between that which was truly received from apostolic teaching and that which found its source in error.[127]

Eventually, through cross influence—through regional gatherings of church leaders and writings of influential individuals—a general agreement began to materialize about which writings were authoritative, based on the above criteria. This process came to a completion in the 4th century, and the Canon has been considered closed since that time.

> The Canon has been considered closed since the 4th century.

The church today is too far removed in time from the original sources to make any significant contribution to the process. A pertinent question today is: "Did the early Christians believe a particular writing was authoritative?" The answer of the early church is that the twenty-seven books that comprise the NT today are the uniquely authorized books for the church.

The following is a sampling of some significant things the early church writers had to say about the authoritative writings. It is beyond the scope of this book to exhaustively layout all that they wrote on this subject. However, this will give the reader a feel for their thoughts.

SOME HIGHLIGHTS FROM THE CHURCH FATHERS IN THE EAST

The first big schism in the church was along an East/West divide. The tensions began and grew in the early centuries, though it is generally agreed that the division was not complete until about 1054. Of particular interest in the study of the Canon is the general agreement about which books were recognized as authoritative between the eastern and western churches.

The church fathers frequently quoted the apostolic writings. However, it needs to be pointed out that a writer simply quoting a source does not prove that the referred-to-text was inspired. In fact, church fathers quoted from other sources as well. What their quotations *do* demonstrate is that knowledge of a writing existed prior to the time of quotation—a useful factor for establishing the date and authorship of the quoted writing. In many cases, quotations from apostolic writings are presented as being equivalent to the authority of the OT.

The following are samplings of some of the eastern writers by region in the early centuries:

Serapion of Antioch (AD 200). "For our part, brethren, we receive both Peter and the other apostles as Christ; but as men of experience we reject the writings falsely inscribed with their names, since we know that such were not handed down to us."[128]

Doctrine of Addai (ca. AD 400). "The Law and the Prophets and the Gospel from which you read every day before the people, and the Epistles of Paul which Simon Cephas sent us from the city of Rome, and the Acts of the Twelve Apostles which John the son of Zebedee sent us from Ephesus—from theses writings you shall read in the churches of the Messiah, and besides them nothing else shall you read."[129]

Dionysius (third quarter of the 2nd century) referred frequently to Paul's writings and shows evidence of knowing Revelation.

Athenagoras (AD 177) was the first to elaborate a philosophical defense of the Trinity. He quotes Paul, Matthew, Mark, and John.

Pantaenus (AD 180-192). "Since the Lord, being the apostle of the Almighty, was sent to the Hebrews, Paul, having been sent to the Gentiles, through modesty did not inscribe himself as an apostle of the Hebrews, both because of respect for the Lord and because he wrote to the Hebrews also out of his abundance, being a preacher and apostle for the Gentiles."[130]

Clement of Alexandria (ca. AD 211) cited all the NT books except Philemon, James, 2 Peter, and 2 and 3 John. The ones he cited he considered authoritative.

Origen (writing early to mid 3rd century). Some have suggested Origen was the first true Christian scholar. He commented on nearly all the NT books, referred to the "New Testament" as "divine Scriptures," and stated that the four gospel accounts were undisputed.

Origen also saw as authoritative Acts, the Pauline epistles (13), 1 Peter, 1 John, and Revelation. However, he viewed the following as disputed: 2 Peter, 2 and 3 John, James, and Jude. He acknowledged that the book of James was written by the Lord's brother. He himself thought Hebrews was authentic and written by Paul but recognized that some churches didn't accept it. He admitted that its authorship is uncertain, suggesting the possibility that it was written under the influence of Paul by someone in Rome, perhaps Luke or Clement of Rome. And he quoted from Hebrews more than two hundred times. Origen treated Didache, the epistle of Barnabas, and the Shepherd of Hermas as authoritative.

SOME HIGHLIGHTS FROM THE CHURCH FATHERS IN THE WEST[131]

Justin Martyr (taught in Rome 150-165). Martyr converted in AD 130, founded a Christian school in Rome, and became a prolific writer. He wrote the following description of a worship service:

> "The memoirs of apostles or the writings of the prophets are read, for as long as time permits. Then the reading stops and the leader instructs by word of mouth, and exhorts to the imitation of these good things. Then we all stand up together and pray."

He quotes from all four gospels and alludes to other writings or oral traditions about the life of Christ.[132]

Irenaeus. In AD 178 Irenaeus became bishop in Lyons. He died ca. AD 202. He was influenced in his youth by Polycarp, who had known the apostle John[133] and some others who had seen the Lord. He was linked with a broad spectrum of churches in diverse areas. Irenaeus made full use of the accepted writings (what we call NT writings) in opposition to Gnosticism. Bruce writes:

> "Irenaeus set himself to examine such claims and to establish the content of the genuine apostolic tradition. This tradition was maintained in living power, he argued, in those churches which were founded by apostles and in which there had been a regular succession of bishops or elders since their foundation; it was summed up in those churches' rule of faith or baptismal creed."[134]

In confronting false teachings, Irenaeus argued that the burden of proof lay with those who asserted that the generally accepted doctrine had changed since the original message (as reflected in the apostolic churches). He claimed that the "rule of faith" was consistent throughout the churches as a whole and did in fact represent the original teachings.

Irenaeus acknowledged that the four-fold gospel was widely accepted. He referred to Paul's epistles, Acts, 1 John, 1 Peter, and Revelation as Scripture. But he also included the Shepherd of Hermas as Scripture. He quoted 2 John and James. In total, he acknowledged as authoritative twenty-two books of what we call the NT.[135]

> Irenaeus was the first to clearly define a collection of apostolic books that were to be regarded as equal in significance to the OT.

Irenaeus was the first to clearly define a collection of apostolic books that were to be regarded as equal in significance to the OT. He implied that inspiration took place even at the word level (in choosing one word over another).

During this time the authoritative writings began circulating in Latin, the common language of Irenaeus's day.[136]

Hippolytus of Rome (AD 170-235). Hippolytus is considered to be the last of the Greek-writing figures in Rome and the greatest scholar of his age in the West.[137] He disagreed with the bishop of Rome over an issue of church discipline and was part of a dissident group against the Roman church establishment.

Hippolytus accepted the four gospels as Scripture, the thiteen epistles of Paul, Acts, 1 Peter, 1 and 2 John, and Revelation (twenty-two books). He quoted frequently from Hebrews but didn't seem to accept it as Scripture. He was the first Christian writer to reflect a knowledge of 2 Peter, and he alluded to James and Jude. He put the known NT books on the same level of authority as OT Scripture by referring to "the prophets, the Lord, and the apostles" as Scripture.

Tertullian (AD 196-212). Tertullian was the first of the church fathers to write primarily in Latin. He converted in Rome and wrote against Marcion and Valentinus (see below). By his time, most of the NT writings were in circulation in Latin among churches of North Africa. He joined the Montanus sect (see below) in Africa (Carthage) about AD 206.

Tertullian was the first to use the phrase "testaments" to refer to the OT and the NT, as we know them today. In so doing, he put the NT books on equal standing with the OT books.[138] He cites all the NT writings except 2 Peter, James, and 2 and 3 John. Early on he spoke favorably of the Shepherd of Hermas, but later declared it to be apocryphal.

> Tertullian was the first to use the phrase "testaments" to refer to the OT and the NT.

Cyprian (converted 246 and died AD 258). Cyprian was bishop of Carthage in Egypt—one of about 250 bishops in North Africa at that time. He quoted from the four gospels, Paul's epistles, 1 Peter, 1 John, Revelation, but not from Philemon, Hebrews, James, 2 Peter, or 2 and 3 John. Cyprian spoke of Hebrews as being authored by Barnabas but did not consider it Scripture.

Clement of Alexandria. Clement lived in the last quarter of the 2nd century in Alexandria before moving to Asia Minor away from the persecution that occurred in AD 202 (he is not to be confused with Clement of Rome).[139] He found much good in pagan culture (in contrast with Tertullian) and taught that everything that is good is for Christ.

Clement spoke of the OT and the NT, but had nothing to say about the limits of the NT.[140] The Law, the Prophets, and the Gospels formed a united authority. Clement was strongly "traditional" but might be more aptly called a Christian "humanist," having read widely among pagan philosophers, especially Plato.

Jerome (AD 340-420). Jerome is most famous for translating the Hebrew OT into Latin, bypassing the Septuagint (the Greek translation of the OT). This created quite a stir, because prior to that time all translations of the OT had been from the Greek Septuagint rather than the Hebrew OT. He wrote that both Hebrews and Revelation were received by the church as authoritative. About the same time, Augustine of Hippo wrote that some books were accepted on weightier evidence than others.[141]

SIGNIFICANT LISTS OF THE BOOKS OF THE NT

Beginning toward the end of the 2nd century, lists began to be drawn up identifying the authoritative books. A few of the more significant (but by no means the only) ones are:

The Muratorian Canon (late 2nd century†)

This is one of the more comprehensive lists from antiquity. The compiler spoke of two criteria for inclusion: first, the authors of a writing were eyewitnesses or ear-witnesses of the Lord; second, the books were widely read in worship services. He mysteriously included "Wisdom Written by Friends of Solomon" without giving a reason. Carson and Moo state:

> "Though virtually valueless as a guide to the origin of the New Testament books to which it refers, [the Muratorian Canon] reflects the view of the great church in recognizing a New Testament canon not very different from our own. The list is fragmentary, so that Mathew and Mark do not appear; but doubtless they are presupposed, since Luke is referred to as the third gospel, and John as the fourth. Luke is also recognized as the author of 'the acts of all the apostles.'"[142]

Cheltenham Manuscript (about AD 360)

Discovered by Theodor Mommsen in 1885, this text is thought to represent usage of the apostolic texts in North Africa. It lists our present NT books with the exception of Hebrews, James, and Jude.[143]

Athanasius' List (AD 367)

This list, included in a letter apparently intended for the Alexandrian church, was the first list to include exclusively the twenty-seven books of the NT that we have today. As some have noted, this was probably prescriptive (in that a book's inclusion meant that it should be accepted) rather than descriptive (that is, stating what was already the case).

> **Athanasius' list was the first list to include exclusively the twenty-seven books of the NT that we have today.**

Eusebius' Canon (early 4th century)[144]

Eusebius was meticulous, particularly concerning church history.[145] He listed his canon and spoke of all other writings as spurious or illegitimate. He made no specific mention of Hebrews, though. This can easily be

---

† Many modern scholars suggest a later date, into the 4th century.

explained by the fact that he believed Paul wrote Hebrews and as such it was included as one of Paul's epistles (though he recognized that there were other viewpoints).

At the request of Emperor Constantine (ca. AD 330), Eusebius prepared fifty copies of the Christian Scripture for use in the imperial city (Constantinople). All indications point to the belief that these copies included the twenty-seven writings we now accept as the NT.[146] Of interest is that Eusebius describes the writings using a threefold classification: the recognized books, the disputed books, and the rejected books (those advanced by heretics).[147]

The above examples of lists are all from the western churches. In the eastern churches, consolidation took a while longer.[148] However, we may speak of the Canon as having arrived at its present form by the 4th century in the western churches and by the 5th century in the eastern churches.

MURATORIUM CANON (2ND CENTURY)	EUSEBIUS' CANON (4TH CENTURY)
Four Gospels	Four Gospels
Paul's Epistles	Acts
Jude	Paul's Epistles (including Hebrews?)
1 and 2 John	1 Peter
Wisdom Written by Friends of Solomon	1 John
Revelation	Revelation
Apocalypse of Peter *	James *
Shepherd of Hermas *	Jude *
	2 Peter *
	2 and 3 John *
* Indicates these were disputed and not on same level of other books.	* Indicates these were disputed by some, yet ultimately accepted by all.[149]

Conclusion

While the fringes of the Canon were disputed until the 4th century, there was a high degree of unity about the majority of the NT Canon (twenty-two books) within the first two centuries over the whole Christian world. Carson and Moo put it this way:

> "Indeed, it is important to observe that, although there was no ecclesiastical machinery like the medieval papacy to enforce decisions, nevertheless the world-wide church almost universally came to accept the same twenty-seven books. It was not so much that the church selected the canon as that the canon selected itself . . . 'When consideration is given to the diversity in cultural backgrounds and in orientation to the essentials of the Christian faith within the churches, their common agreement about which books belonged to the New Testament serves to suggest that this final decision did not originate solely at the human level.'"[150]

Bruce summarizes the situation well:

> "Although the fringes of the emerging canon remained unsettled for generations, a high degree of unanimity concerning the greater part of the NT was attained among the very diverse and scattered congregations of believers not only throughout the Mediterranean world but also over an area extending from Britain to Mesopotamia. By the end of the third century and the beginning of the fourth century, the great majority of the twenty-seven books that still later came to be widely regarded as the canonical NT was almost universally acknowledged to be authoritative."[151]

Chapter Nine

The Non-Canonical Writings

As we have seen, the NT documents did not arise in a vacuum. Many other literary works existed, some arising before the time of the apostles, and some after. It is to these we now turn to get an overview of what they were all about.

The Apocrypha

Introduction

The subject of the Apocrypha (or deutero-canonical books as Roman Catholicism would term them) bears on the development of the NT Canon. The developing Christian community wrestled with whether to adopt some of the apocryphal books. To this day there is some disagreement as to their importance, with some Bible editions including these extra books with varying degrees of acceptance of their assumed authority.

> The term *apocrypha* comes from a Greek word that means "hidden" or "concealed."

The term *apocrypha* comes from a Greek word that means "hidden" or "concealed." It was applied by some of the early church fathers (for example, Origen, Irenaeus, and Jerome) to a specific collection of books as a way of distinguishing them from the canonical books of the OT.[152]

A brief history of the Apocrypha

The Hebrew OT was translated in Egypt between 250 and 150 BC into Greek, the common language among Jews living in Egypt at that time. This translation is called the Septuagint, also referred to as the LXX. Legend has it that the LXX was the work of seventy-two Jewish elders (six from each tribe) brought to Alexandria to perform the translation.[153] The legend goes on to say that these scholars completed the translation of the Pentateuch (the first five books of the OT) in seventy-two days and produced seventy-two identical versions from separate cells in isolation from each other. Later the legend expanded to apply it to all of the Hebrew OT. In reality, we know very little about how the Septuagint came into being.[154]

> The Hebrew OT was translated into Greek . . . this translation is called the Septuagint.

At some unknown point in its history, the writings which we call the Apocrypha were added to the Septuagint beyond the thirty-nine books accepted by the Jews. Their inclusion most likely occurred sometime *after* the time of Christ and His apostles. Some have suggested that it was the rise of the codex form of book production at the end of the 1st century which led to the apocryphal books being included with early editions of the Septuagint.

The earliest actual manuscript evidence of the apocryphal books comes to us from the 4th century AD by way of Codex Vaticanus and Codex Sinaiticus. These two manuscripts both include the Greek OT and the canonical books of the NT as well as some of the apocryphal books, though not the same ones. However, both of these copies came decidedly from within the Christian community and tell us nothing about whether the apocryphal books were included in the Greek Scriptures used by the Jews during the time of Jesus and the apostles.

These apocryphal writings were obviously considered worthy of copying, but they were never part of the Hebrew canonical OT and were never accepted by the Jews as authoritative or inspired. In fact, a Jewish Council held in AD 90 made a determinative pronouncement that recognized only the books now in the Hebrew Bible. The apocryphal books were specifically not included.

The early church. During the expansion of Christianity, the LXX became the OT edition of choice for Gentile converts, since for the most part they were Greek-speaking. The growing antagonism between Jews and Christians led to the Jews abandoning the Greek LXX in favor of the Hebrew OT. The result is that almost all copies of the LXX surviving from antiquity were copied by Christians.

As mentioned above, at some point the apocryphal books were added to the LXX. We don't know how early these were added, but the latest date for doing so would have been the 4th century AD (as reflected in the two early manuscripts above).

As Latin came into greater usage, the need for translation of the LXX into Latin became apparent. Jerome, however, in his 4th century translation, the Vulgate, went back to the original Hebrew rather than the Greek LXX. He held that translating directly from the Hebrew would be more accurate than (and superior to) translating from a Greek translation of the Hebrew original. Though he included the apocryphal books in his translation, he distinguished between them and the authoritative books of the Hebrew OT. However, he did consider those apocryphal books profitable for their ethical lessons.

Augustine (AD 354-430), a contemporary of Jerome, felt on the other hand that the Greek LXX should be given as much if not more authority than the Hebrew edition. He also saw the apocryphal books as authoritative because of their seeming widespread use.[155] In AD 393, a regional council in the city of Hippo (where Augustine was prominent) pronounced a list of canonical books and included the Apocrypha.[156] This was apparently the first council to make a pronouncement on the Canon, but this list was not common to the broader church body.

Since the apocryphal books were included in the Vulgate, they were circulated and read for the better part of one thousand years among the Latin-speaking western churches. However, many of the Greek-speaking church fathers did not include the apocryphal books in their lists of accepted books, and thus lesser emphasis was accorded to them in the eastern churches. It was later, during the Reformation period, that the controversy reached a pinnacle.[157]

These extra books, though considered worthwhile, were never accepted on a par with the rest of the OT, either by the Jews or by the early Christians. Nor were they considered part of the NT by Christians.[158]

The Reformers. Up to the time of the Reformation (the 1500s), the Apocrypha was treated distinctly from the NT. Martin Luther, the most well-known of the reformers, rejected the Apocrypha, following Jerome's (4th century) thinking. He did, however, include it in an appendix at the end of his German translation of the OT. Though Luther agreed there was spiritual value to these writings, he rejected them as uninspired. The rest of the reformers, by and large, also rejected the Apocrypha as not being authoritative.

> Up to the time of the Reformation, the Apocrypha was treated distinctly from the NT.

In response to the reformers' actions, the Roman Catholic Council of Trent (AD 1545-46) set aside Jerome and others' distinction and accepted the Apocrypha as authoritative. From this point onward, the division between those who held the apocryphal books to be authoritative and those who did not became more polarized.

King James Translation (KJV) and onward. The KJV[159] Bible of 1611 included the Apocrypha as an appendix. But in AD 1626 copies of the KJV Bible began to be published without it. In 1644, the Church of England ordered that the Apocrypha should not be read in church services. The Westminster Confession (1646) proclaimed the Apocrypha was not part of the Canon.

With the rise of Bible societies (ca. 1804) the KJV Bible was printed largely without the Apocrypha. Other versions of the Bible that have included the Apocrypha are: New English Bible, Revised English Bible, New Revised Standard Version, Jerusalem Bible, and The New American Bible of 1970.[160] The Apocrypha is not included in many modern translations such as the NASB, RSV, or NIV.

> With the rise of Bible societies, the KJV Bible was printed largely without the Apocrypha.

Today. The Roman Catholic Church continues to hold to the proclamations of the Council of Trent which asserted the authority of the Apocrypha. After listing out what was considered to be the canonical books (which included the sixty-six books of the Bible plus the additional apocryphal books), the council stated:

> "If anyone does not accept as sacred and canonical the aforesaid books in their entirety and with all their parts, as they have been accustomed to be read in the Catholic Church and as they are contained in the old Latin Vulgate Edition, and knowingly and deliberately rejects the aforesaid traditions, let him be anathema."[161]

Clearly, the Roman Catholic Church's stand is quite divisive and calls for the strongest possible condemnation for those who reject the Apocrypha! This is the unchanging stance of the church to this day. However, the point must be made that contemporary Roman Catholicism does, though, maintain a distinction, as F. F. Bruce points out:

> "There is general agreement among Roman Catholic scholars today . . . to call them [the Apocrypha] 'deuterocanonical.' . . . Jerome's distinction is thus maintained in practice."[162]

In other words, the apocryphal books are to be considered secondary, as Jerome insisted in the 4th century. The Orthodox churches (Russian, Greek, Armenian, Ethiopian, etc.) today accept some of the books of the Apocrypha as canonical, although they differ as to which books to include.[163] Protestantism as a whole has rejected the Apocrypha as being non-authoritative, though some segments within Protestantism find value in these books.

Thus, the line of demarcation between Roman Catholicism and Protestantism today still runs down the middle of the debate on the Apocrypha.[164]

> **The line of demarcation between Roman Catholicism and Protestantism today still runs down the middle of the debate on the Apocrypha.**

Writings in the LXX Apocrypha

Although different lists contain variations, the following chart shows the books typically included in the LXX and a brief description of each.[165]

THE APOCRYPHAL BOOKS (LXX)	
BOOK	DESCRIPTION
1 and 2 Esdras	Covers 'history' corresponding to that of 2 Chronicles 35:1 to Nehemiah 8:13.
Tobit, Judith	Reflects life and events during the Assyrian and Babylonian captivity.
Prayer of Azariah and Song of 3 Holy Children, Susanna, Bel and the Dragon	Additions to the story of Daniel.
Esther 10:4-16:25	Additions to the book of Esther (apparently to add a spiritual aspect to what otherwise seemed to be lacking).
Epistle of Manasseh	Corresponding to 2 Chronicles 33:10-13.
Epistle of Jeremiah	A letter ostensibly written by Jeremiah.
Baruch	Corresponding to Jeremiah 1:14.
Ecclesiasticus/Sirach (also called The Wisdom of Jesus)	A collection of proverbs similar to the canonical book of Proverbs.
Wisdom of Solomon	A general work on the benefits of wisdom.
1 and 2 Maccabbees	Historical events in the inter-testamental period.
Psalm 151	An addition to the OT Psalter.

Reasons for rejecting the Apocrypha

It may seem persuasive that the majority of Christendom (in the form of the Roman Catholic Church and the Orthodox churches) holds that the evidence weighs in favor of including some or all of the apocryphal books as authoritative, albeit on a secondary level. However, the majority is not always right. One must study the circumstances surrounding these books and apply the same standards to them that led to the recognition of the twenty-seven canonical books. By such standards, the apocryphal books are not to be accepted, despite the contrary dogma of the majority.

A summary of some arguments against accepting the Apocrypha (deutero-canonical) as canonical are as follows:[†]

1) The apocryphal books were not considered by the Jews to be part of the canonical OT.

2) Contrary to popular assertions, there is no historical evidence that these books were part of the OT Scriptures (Septuagint) that Jesus and the apostles used.

3) The first historical evidence of the inclusion of the apocryphal books with the Scriptures comes relatively late (the 4th century AD) and comes from within the Christian community. This says nothing about whether it was included by the Jews in the Septuagint before that.

4) The apocryphal books were not written by acknowledged OT prophets (not withstanding the implied claim of some to be additions to other OT books). And since they predated the time of Christ, they fail the test of apostolicity.

5) There was clearly not a unanimous testimony among the early church fathers about their authority. For example, Jerome did not accept them as authoritative. Others, rejecting them, include such noted fathers as Origen and Athanasius. Even among those who ascribed authority to the apocryphal books, there was wide disagreement as to which books to include. No general council of all the churches included these books in their list of canonical books for nearly the first four centuries. Therefore these books failed one of the basic tests of canonicity, namely, universal acceptance.

6) Alleged quotes in the NT to apocryphal books lend no more support to their canonicity than quotes to other non-biblical writings, such as the Book of Enoch (Jude 14) which Roman Catholics do not accept as deutero-canonical or Greek philosophical writings which Paul alludes to, for example, in Acts 17:28 and Titus 1:12.

[†] For a fuller presentation of this discussion, see Norman L. Geisler and Ralph E. MacKenzie, *Roman Catholics and Evangelicals: Agreements and Differences* (Grand Rapids, MI: Baker Book House, 1995), 157-175.

7) Though there may be some allusions in the NT to apocryphal books, no apocryphal book is ever cited as scripture or cited in any authoritative sense.

8) Even the Council of Trent's (AD 1546) listing of deutero-canonical books differed from what many of the early church fathers held.

9) Some of the apocryphal books contain demonstrable historical errors, inaccuracies, and obvious inconsistencies,[167] as well as contradictory theological perspectives, such as praying for the dead (2 Maccabbees 12:40-45, contrast with Hebrews 9:27).

Is the Apocrypha useful for Christians today?

Historical value. The apocryphal books are useful as additional source material for understanding the historical and cultural background of biblical times. The books of the Maccabbees, for instance, contribute to our understanding of the history of the inter-testamental times, between the last of the Jewish prophets and the coming of the Messiah. We must remember that if we conclude that the apocryphal books are not authoritative, we should be cautious about any uncorroborated renderings of history we find in them.

Spiritual value. Some in the early church did find spiritual value in the apocryphal books, just as they did with other non-canonical writings, like the Shepherd of Hermas. Compare them to Christians today reading books such as *Pilgrim's Progress* or Christian historical novels. While there might be some spiritual value for devotional reading, we must be cautious that we don't give more weight to them than to any other book written by mere human authors.

DUBIOUS WRITINGS[168]

In addition to the Apocrypha, other books circulated and were accorded various degrees of authority by different groups and sects. Some were purportedly biographies of the life of Christ, while others were histories, letters, and apocalypses (end-time prophecies).

> The early believers were curious about two areas of Jesus' life (His infancey and childhood and the period between His death and resurrection).

Other Gospels

There were two kinds of "gospel accounts." First there were those designed to *supplement* the four apostolic gospels. The early believers were curious about two areas of Jesus' life (His infancy and childhood and the period between His death and resurrection) of which little if anything is mentioned in the canonical gospels. Only one incident is recorded, and that depicts Jesus as a young boy in the temple (Luke 2:41-51). The dubious gospels often purported to depict the omitted events.

Second, there were gospels designed to *supplant* the four gospels. These were written by sects to shore up their theological viewpoints. None of these writings established themselves.

Some examples of these spurious gospels are:

- ➤ ***Fragments of an Unknown Gospel*** (AD 110-30). These include incidents not recorded in the canonical gospels. Only fragments have survived the years, "the historical value of which was of slender proportions at best."[169]

- ➤ ***Gospel of the Hebrews*** (mid 2nd century). Written in a Semitic language, not Greek, this writing was used somewhat among the early Christians until the 4th century. Only fragments come down to us today, as most of it was lost. It differed considerably from the four canonical gospels in substance and character.

- ➤ ***Gospel of the Egyptians*** (sometime after AD 150). Accepted as canonical by some churches in parts of Egypt, only a few fragments are preserved. It promoted doctrines like the rejection of marriage and gender egalitarianism.

- ➤ ***Gospel of Peter*** (mid 2nd century). Origen, and later Eusebius, casually refers to it, which is why we know of its existence. One small fragment believed to be of this writing was discovered in 1886.

- ➤ ***Various Others.*** Protoevangelium of James, Infancy Story of Thomas, Arabic Infancy Gospel, Armenian Gospel of the Infancy, History of Joseph the Carpenter, Gospel of the Birth of Mary, Gospel of Nicodemus, Gospel of Bartholomew (refers to Jesus' visit to Hades).

Histories (called "Acts")

Popular histories arose claiming to report certain activities of the apostles following the resurrection of Christ. Metzger points out,

> "These several books of 'Acts', the contents of which have only the most meager historical basis, resemble in some respects the Graeco-Roman novels of the period, though replacing the obscenities of many of these with moralizing calculated to provide instruction in Christian piety."[170]

Some of the more popular histories that purportedly concerned the apostolic movement are the following:

- ➤ *Acts of Paul.* A romance novel written about AD 170 by a priest in Rome claimed to honor Paul by reporting on unpublished facts about his ministry. Though the book was popular, the author was put on trial by his peers and convicted of falsifying the facts.
- ➤ *Acts of Peter.* Written in the latter half of the 2nd century, this work contains the *Quo Vadis* legend in which Jesus allegedly met Peter as the apostle was on his way to being crucified upside down.
- ➤ *Acts of John.* Supposedly an eyewitness account of John's missionary efforts, this work was composed around the close of the 2nd century.
- ➤ *Less popular* were the Acts of Andrew, Thomas, Philip, Andrew and Matthias, Bartholomew, Thaddeus, Barnabas (all found to be written between the 2nd and 4th centuries).

Epistles (letters)

Various other writings emerged in the early centuries that were purportedly written under apostolic authority but which were rejected by the church. The following are a sample:

- ➤ *The Epistle of the Apostles* (AD 180).
- ➤ *Third Epistle of Paul to the Corinthians,*[171] which was actually included as part of the Acts of Paul, written in AD 170.
- ➤ *Epistle to the Laodiceans,* probably written at the close of the 3rd century.

> *Correspondence between Paul and the Roman philosopher Seneca* (14 letters), with an uncertain date of authorship.

Apocalypses (end time prophecies)
> *Of Peter* (AD 125-150).
> *Of Paul* (AD 250).

Miscellaneous writings

Some of the writings of the apostolic fathers[172] were accepted as authoritative for a time. But when lists of canonical books began to solidify, these were all left out. Some of these include the following:

> *Didache* (accepted through the 3rd century in some churches).
> *Epistle of Clement* (read in public worship in AD 170).[173]
> *Epistle of Barnabas* (considered fringe).
> *The Shepherd of Hermas* (accepted into the 3rd century by some, but later universally rejected).

Gnostic writings

A whole separate class of writings arose in support of the Gnostic movement. Examples of these are the following:

Gospel of Thomas (ca. AD 140). This work begins: "These are the secret words which the living Jesus spoke and (which) Didymus Judas Thomas wrote down." It contains 114 lines, almost all of which are introduced by the words "Jesus said" (some of which have a Gnostic twist). "The strongest claims for authenticity have been made on behalf of the Gospel of Thomas, which, strictly speaking, is not a 'gospel' at all but a collection of . . . sayings of Jesus."[174] While some assert that Gnostic gospels such as this one are more primitive than the canonical gospels, few hold to this view.

Gospel of Philip (2nd century). This is a collection of disjointed excerpts emphasizing Gnostic theology. It alludes to the gospels of Matthew and John, and also to the epistle of 1 John. It also reflects an acquaintance with Romans, 1 and 2 Corinthians, Galatians, and Philippians.

Exegesis of the Soul (ca. AD 200), which quotes from the OT and the NT, promotes asceticism, and quotes three times from Homer's *Odyssey*.

Apocryphon of James (2nd or 3rd century), which contains questions and answers between Jesus and His disciples and a few references or allusions to the NT books.

Others: Treatise on Resurrection, Trimorphic Protennoia, Hypostasis of the Archon, Epistle of Peter to Philip.

Although some today have popularized the Gnostic view of early Christianity, the church thoroughly rejected these writings because of their late date and their obvious lack of apostolic authority.

Chapter Ten

The Canon and Church Authority

The study of the NT Canon surfaces a core dispute between Roman Catholic (RC) and Protestant scholars. The challenge is made by RC scholars: "If Protestants accept the authority of the early church in determining the Canon, how can they reject that same authority when it comes to the doctrines of apostolic succession and the Eucharist?" This is a contentious issue because the RC Church believes in the primacy of the pope and the authority of the church as a whole—which they trace through an unbroken line of apostolic succession stretching back to the apostle Peter. So the assertion is that the issue of authority of the NT documents is inextricably wound up with the authority of the early church, and subsequently with the RC Church. Catholic theologian Nicolaus Appel summarizes as follows: "Must not Protestant principles be surrounded with uncertainty and a consciousness of the church's fallibility even in the recognition of the canon? Such questions have initiated a crisis in Protestantism that to the present day remains unsolved."[175]

> The study of the NT Canon surfaces a core dispute between Roman Catholic and Protestant scholars.

Of course, it is not at all clear that there *is* such a crisis, except in the minds of those who wish to prove Protestantism in error at the most fundamental level. There are a number of satisfactory responses to this concern.

101

Differences Over the Extent of the Incarnation

At the core of this issue is the *extent* of the incarnation. All Christians believe that God the Son was incarnated in a human body in the person of Jesus of Nazareth, and that He was the Messiah (Christ) foretold in the OT. However, Roman Catholicism goes further and holds that since the day of Pentecost, Christ has been incarnated in the church, the living body of Christ. Further, according to RC teaching, in the same way that the Holy Spirit was active in Jesus when He was here on earth, He is now active in and through the church. While biblically it is true that Christ does indwell all believers (Col. 1:27), and that the Holy Spirit works through us (Col. 1:29), the Roman Catholic Church takes this in a much more literal sense and applies it to the corporate body. Attending this is the belief, therefore, that the corporate church has the authority of Christ and that the Spirit works infallibly through the church (at least at certain times). If this is true, then what the Spirit does, He does infallibly—including guiding the church to recognize the Canon of the NT. Appel says, "Only on the ground of an infallibly guided church can there be a sure canon."[176] Consistent with this line of thought, the Roman Catholic Church tells us that we must also accept that the Spirit worked infallibly in the early church's teaching on apostolic succession.

In response, Protestantism sees the incarnation being expressed exclusively in the Person of Jesus Christ, there being no convincing evidence from Scripture to suggest otherwise. To be sure, the Spirit of God lives in all true believers, but the idea that the church as a body of believers is therefore infallible is unknown in Scripture. Additionally, if the so-called doctrine of apostolic succession (in the sense of passing on the authority of the apostles) is as foundational as Roman Catholic dogma teaches, one would think the Spirit would have made this very clear in the NT documents themselves! But this is not the case.

Following the RC Church's teaching as stated above, we would well ask the question: Does the RC Church believe that everything the church teaches is infallible? If the Spirit was working infallibly in the early church, at what point did the witness of the Spirit *become* infallible? Though tongue-in-cheek, the point is that the church endured much disagreement in the first four centuries over the extent of the Canon, and only settled things at various councils. Clearly, the Spirit must have not been working infallibly in the corporate church at times!

A biblical case-in-point will help make this clear. Peter, whom the RC Church holds to be the first pope and therefore the first in apostolic succession, wrote two letters that are included in the NT Canon (1 Peter and 2 Peter). God used him to pen a portion of inspired—and therefore infallible—Scripture. We even take it from the words of Peter's inspired text that Paul was also the author of inspired Scripture:

> ". . . regard the patience of our Lord as salvation; just as also our beloved brother Paul, according to the wisdom given him, wrote to you, as also in all his letters, speaking in them of these things, in which are some things hard to understand, which the untaught and unstable distort, as they do also the rest of the Scriptures, to their own destruction." (2 Peter 3:15-16)

At one and the same time, Peter puts Paul's writings on the same level as "the rest of the Scriptures," and also warns about false teachers who distort the Scriptures. According to RC logic, we would expect that since Peter was the first in apostolic succession and that he was used by God to write inspired Scripture, then he must be right in all he practiced. This is the same argument as saying that if God used the church to recognize the NT Canon, then He worked infallibly in the church practice of taking apostolic authority as dogmatic truth. However, this does not follow in Peter's case, the supposed first pope. Hear what Paul says about an incident in which Peter practiced hypocrisy:

> "But when Cephas [i.e. Peter] came to Antioch, I opposed him to his face, because he *stood condemned*. For prior to the coming of certain men from James, he used to eat with the Gentiles; but when they came, he began to withdraw and hold himself aloof, fearing the party of the circumcision. The rest of the Jews joined him in hypocrisy, with the result that even Barnabas was carried away by *their hypocrisy*. But when I saw that they were not straightforward about the truth of the gospel, I said to Cephas in the presence of all, 'If you, being a Jew, live like the Gentiles and not like the Jews, how is it that you compel the Gentiles to live like Jews? We are Jews by nature and not sinners from among the Gentiles; nevertheless knowing that a man is not justified by the works of the Law but through faith in Christ Jesus, even we have believed in Christ Jesus, so that we may be justified by faith in Christ and not by the works of the Law; since by the works of the Law no flesh will be justified.'" (Gal. 2:11-16, emphasis added)

God used human means when it came to writing the canonical text, yet at times that writing recorded the error of Peter (as described harshly by the apostle Paul). In the same way, God used the early church when it came to identifying what was truly canonical, yet it was also possible (indeed probable) that at other times the church practiced error. And I believe that is the case when it comes to apostolic succession and other early (and later) church errors. We conclude, therefore, that there is no inconsistency in the Protestant rejection of apostolic succession or other early church aberrations from biblical doctrine.

THE NATURE OF CANONICITY

Related to this discussion of church authority is the nature of canonicity. We have shown elsewhere that the Canon did not derive its authority from the decision or authority of the early church. It is not the case that the writings were drifting around with no divine authority until the church rescued them and elevated them to canonical status with divine authority (implying that if the church had not done so, the writings would have remained the mere scratchings of men).

But that was not what happened. What *did* happen was that the writings which came to be recognized as canonical were imbued with divine authority apart from any recognition by the church—the church councils merely identified what was *already* divinely authoritative. Of significant interest is the fact that the Canon in its general form was secured long before any of the 4th century councils declared on this matter. One scholar puts it this way: "The apparent spontaneous development of the canon suggests that it is more appropriate to speak of a *recognition* rather than a selection of the New Testament books."[177]

> Church councils merely identified what was *already* divinely authoritative.

The present-day study of the Canon is an *historical investigation* into what the early church recognized as truly apostolic. They were in a much better chronological proximity for determining what was apostolic and what was not than we are today.

Now it is probably true that the NT documents themselves may not have originally been received as *canonical*. Remember, the concern of a NT Canon developed over time—that is why we speak of the authority of the writings in the earliest church history as opposed to canonicity, which came more clearly over time. Dunbar writes,

> "The process by which the written form of that witness [i.e. apostolic] rose to increasing prominence and was gradually defined in the canonical understanding of the church was both natural and spontaneous. The process was, to a great extent, underway before the Christian community was aware of its implications . . . The recognition of this apostolicity, moreover, was based primarily on the tradition of the church. Those books that had functioned authoritatively for earlier Christians were received as an authentic apostolic tradition. In turn, those documents were used in a negative way to exclude works of later vintage or varying doctrinal content, as happened, for example, in the case of *The Gospel of Peter*."[178]

Herman Ridderbos gives this interesting sense to the matter when he writes,

> "The Church has dealt in this situation as does one who knows and points to a certain person as father and mother. Such a knowledge rests not on demonstration but upon direct experience; it is most closely connected with one's own identify. In this and no other way must we picture the knowledge and the 'decision' of the Church concerning the canon."[179]

So we conclude that the church was not acting infallibly in "determining" which documents were to be given divine authority. Rather, the church merely recognized which documents God had already divinely inspired. As mentioned above, the early church was better situated to make that determination; we are too far removed in time to either add to or take away from their discussion.

THE RELATION TO ALL DOCTRINES AND DOGMAS

Having established the nature of the canonical process, we now have the authoritative texts, namely, the NT documents,

> Canonicity is absolutely foundational to all doctrine and is established without appeal to the church's authority.

against which we may (and must!) evaluate all doctrines and dogmas of the church. Determining the nature of the Canon is a different category of investigation than determining the doctrines of the faith. Canonicity is absolutely foundational to all doctrine and is established without appeal to the church's authority. All doctrines are established by appealing solely to those authoritative texts, the NT documents. There is no contradiction or crisis. We can consistently accept the early church's perspective on canonicity on historical grounds without feeling compelled to accept the early church's erroneous teaching on theological grounds in other areas of the Christian faith, in particular, regarding apostolic succession.

To be sure, the element of faith is needed in all this, but this view is internally consistent with the canonical writings themselves.[180] In the final analysis we echo the common Protestant rejoinder: "The Canon is not the product of the church; rather, the church is a product of the Canon."

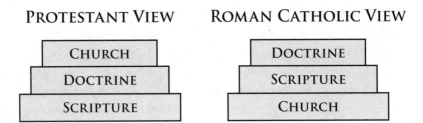

Chapter Eleven

Formatting the Texts

The study of the development of book titles and chapter and verse divisions is not properly part of the study of canonicity, but the topic satisfies some curiosity at this juncture. As copies of the original writings began circulating and the veneration for them grew, the church increasingly referred to them in congregational teachings and recitations. The need became apparent for a consistent way of identifying and locating passages. Styles and conventions of writing changed as well, so a consistent pattern was devised for formatting copies so as to be usable for subsequent generations of listeners and readers. Thus, word renderings, punctuation, versifications, and book titles became necessary.

> The need became apparent for a consistent way of identifying and locating passages.

Words and Punctuation

The character forms of the actual original writings are uncertain since the original documents no longer exist. However, it was normal for the common Greek of the early church era to be written without capital letters, punctuation, or even spaces between the words. Some of our earliest manuscripts exhibit these characteristics. Punctuation marks and capitalizations did not appear in the texts until the 6th and 7th centuries, in keeping with later language conventions. It follows, therefore, that punctuation in neither the Greek text nor the translations is part of the original documents. One ramification of this is that, consistent with Greek convention, a simple statement can be translated as a statement of fact or as a question, depending on the context. Scholars are able to determine and place punctuation based on contextual and interpretative concerns. Also, contrary to the convention in some English Bibles today, the original Greek did not capitalize the first letter of names or pronouns referring to God.

Figure 4. An example of early MSS formatting. Codex Sinaiticus, ca 4th century. Owned by the British Library, London. Used by permission of the Center for the Study of New Testament Documents.

Chapter Divisions

Early copies did not have chapter or verse divisions, or any other aids to locate specific teachings or passages. In time, copyists found it practical to provide some markings to help the readers identify locations of lines of texts. Various methods were used, but a standard form was quite a time in coming.

The first record we have of chapter divisions becoming standard was in the Latin Vulgate, around 1100. This scheme subsequently became the basis for the English chapter divisions.[181]

Verse Divisions

Verse markings were first added to the Greek and Latin editions in 1551 and quickly found their way into the English editions. Little is known about the rationale behind the specific verse divisions, some of which admittedly seem arbitrary to us today.

Titles of the Books

Generally speaking, titles were not as important among ancient writings as they have been since the time of the printing press. Thus the original autographs of the canonical writings probably did not contain titles. When titles did begin to appear, the opening words of a book served to identify its contents. After that, there is considerable variance in thus identifying canonical writings, even among today's modern editions.

The Gospels. As the four canonical gospels were collected and circulated, the need became apparent to distinguish between them. Since all were considered "the gospel,"[182] the distinguishing characteristic had to do with identifying whose perspective was being presented. Thus the words "According to . . ." were added to the author's name to form the titles. In time, the characterization of the four books as gospel accounts came to be included in the titles: "The Gospel According to Matthew," etc. What was universally clear was that there were not four different gospel accounts, but one which was simply presented by four different writers.

The Acts of the Apostles. The title reflects the historical content of the book, being a sequel to the Gospels—namely, the events surrounding the spread of Christianity after the resurrection and ascension of Christ. The primary focus is on the ministries of the apostles Peter and Paul. When this title became affixed to the book is uncertain, but it seems to have been present from early times.

The Epistles of Paul. The collection of Paul's letters was from early times introduced by the title "The Epistles of Paul," with the individual letters entitled, for example, "To the Romans," etc. These eventually gave way to titles such as "The epistle of Paul to the Romans."

General Epistles. These followed somewhat the convention of Paul's epistles, with the titles changing and evolving. Generally, the titles included the author and/or the recipients.

Revelation. The earliest titles of this book contained the words "The Revelation of John," which reflect the recipient of the revelation detailed therein. The later title "The Revelation of Jesus Christ" mirrored the opening verses of the book, which focus more on the *content* of the revelation.

ORDER OF THE BOOKS

Historically, the order of canonical books varied from list to list.

The Gospels. It was natural that the four gospels were kept together since they were considered to be essentially one gospel rendered in four different ways. Because of the centrality of the person of Jesus Christ to Christianity, the Gospels, being the authorized biographies of Jesus Christ, were usually found at the beginning of most lists of the canonical books.

> Because of the centrality of Jesus Christ to Christianity, the Gospels were usually found at the beginning of most lists of the canonical books.

The current ordering of the accounts (Matthew, Mark, Luke, and John) occurs almost universally in the ancient Greek manuscripts and dates back at least to the time of Jerome. This was the order adopted by Eusebius when he produced his fifty copies in the 4th century. It has been largely followed in subsequent manuscripts. This order is hinted at in the Muratorian Canon (late 2nd century) which referred to Luke and John as the third and forth gospels respectively.

The Acts of the Apostles. Being the historical sequel to Christ's earthly life and ministry, it is easy to see why Acts usually followed immediately after the Gospels. This is similar to the OT pattern where the historical books were grouped together following the Pentateuch, which is the heart of the OT.[183]

The General Epistles. These are the writings of James, Peter, John, and Jude. Almost all the ancient Greek manuscripts placed these letters immediately after Acts and before Paul's letters.[184] This Greek ordering may have reflected the closer proximity of the writers to Jesus in His historical ministry and thus given a favored status in book order. Two of these four writers were part of the "inner circle" of Jesus' disciples (John and Peter),[185] and three of them were viewed as "pillars" of the church (see Galatians 2:9). Also, the early church may have thought that these Epistles had a more wide-spread audience, and because of this given them priority over Paul's letters, which were written to specific churches or individuals.[186] In time this sub-collection was moved to its current location just before the Book of Revelation.

> Paul's writings circulated from the earliest times as a single collection, so it was natural that they were kept together in most lists.

Epistles of Paul. Paul's writings circulated from the earliest times as a single collection, so it was natural that they were kept together in most lists. By the time of the English translations, the epistles of Paul were generally placed before the General Epistles. Possibly this was because of the doctrinal importance of Paul's writings. The reason for the specific ordering within Paul's writings is uncertain. However, some observations are in order:

- ➤ His letters to churches are listed before his letters to individuals.
- ➤ His letters are grouped according to their recipients. So, for example, the two epistles to the Corinthian church are kept together.
- ➤ Longer letters are generally placed ahead of shorter letters.
- ➤ Possibly the epistle to the Romans was placed first because of its length and because it seems to be Paul's doctrinal treatise on his core teaching of justification by faith.

The Epistle to the Hebrews. Although scholars today are uncertain of the authorship of Hebrews, it was often included with the collection of

Paul's letters in the first few centuries. With a few exceptions, it was usually placed last among Paul's writings following Philemon.

The Book of the Revelation. This book was normally listed last, which seems fitting in light of its forward-looking nature.

The present ordering of the NT books is therefore laid out very systematically, as seen in the following table:

New Testament Book Order	
Four Gospels	Jesus Christ.
Acts of the Apostles	Historical sequal, biography of sorts of the apostles.
Paul's Letters and Hebrews	From the earliest times, these circulated as a single group.
General Letters	Include letters written by Peter, James, John, and Jude.
The Book of the Revelation	Capstone of NT writings that enables Christians to preview future events.

CHAPTER TWELVE

PUTTING IT ALL TOGETHER

Concluding that the canonical NT books are historically authentic, we can now use these writings themselves, along with the other historical writings at our disposal, to help piece together the development of the Canon of the NT. We begin with the teachings of the Lord Jesus Christ himself.

JESUS CHRIST TAUGHT THAT HIS WORDS WERE AUTHORITATIVE AND ON THE LEVEL OF OT SCRIPTURES

"'Therefore everyone who hears these words of Mine and acts on them, may be compared to a wise man who built his house on the rock. And the rain fell, and the floods came, and the winds blew and slammed against that house; and yet it did not fall, for it had been founded on the rock. Everyone who hears these words of Mine and does not act on them, will be like a foolish man who built his house on the sand. The rain fell, and the floods came, and the winds blew and slammed against that house; and it fell—and great was its fall.' When Jesus had finished these words, the crowds were amazed at His teaching; for He was teaching them as one having authority, and not as their scribes." (Matt. 7:24-29)

"For truly I say to you, until heaven and earth pass away, not the smallest letter or stroke shall pass from the Law until all is accomplished." (Matt. 5:18)

113

"Heaven and earth will pass away, but My words will not pass away." (Matt. 24:35)

JESUS CHRIST MADE PROVISION FOR THE PROPAGATION OF HIS TEACHINGS

He authorized the apostles to be His official witnesses, to convey His teachings to others.

". . . you [i.e. apostles] shall be My witnesses both in Jerusalem, and in all Judea and Samaria, and even to the remotest part of the earth." (Acts 1:8)

He promised them supernatural ability to recall His teachings.

"But the Helper, the Holy Spirit, whom the Father will send in My name, He will teach you all things, and bring to your remembrance all that I said to you." (John 14:26)

He promised that further truth would be revealed to them (truth He did not specifically teach prior to Pentecost).

"I have many things to say to you, but you cannot bear them now. But when He, the Spirit of truth comes, He will guide you into all the truth; for He will not speak on His own initiative, but whatever He hears, He will speak; and He will disclose to you what is to come." (John 16:12-13)

The eleven apostles understood the importance of Jesus' instructions.

They considered it necessary to add a replacement apostle after Judas's betrayal to bring the number of authorized witnesses back to twelve. Peter spoke what they all knew to be the case:

"Therefore it is necessary that of the men who have accompanied us all the time that the Lord Jesus went in and out among us—beginning with the baptism of John until the day that He was taken up from us—one of these must become a witness with us of His resurrection." (Acts 1:21-23)

THE DISCIPLES WERE CONVINCED THAT JESUS DID RISE FROM THE DEAD

The disciples were initially skeptical about Christ's resurrection but became absolutely confident once they saw Him in person.

> The disciples were initially skeptical about Christ's resurrection but became absolutely confident once they saw Him in person.

"While they were telling these things, He Himself stood in their midst and said to them, 'Peace be to you.' But they were startled and frightened and thought that they were seeing a spirit. And He said to them, 'Why are you troubled, and why do doubts arise in your hearts? See My hands and My feet, that it is I Myself; touch Me and see, for a spirit does not have flesh and bones as you see that I have.' And when He had said this, He showed them His hands and His feet. While they still could not believe it because of their joy and amazement, He said to them, 'Have you anything here to eat?' They gave Him a piece of a broiled fish; and He took it and ate it before them." (Luke 24:36-43)

Notice, they thought they saw a ghost, but then Jesus verified that His presence was physical by inviting them to touch Him and to eat with Him. They were transformed from depressed, defeated, and fearful men following the death of Christ into men of great courage and conviction following His resurrection.

In Peter's grand Pentecost message to the masses, in order to support the physical resurrection of Christ, he contrasts the historical fact that David died and stayed dead with the fact of Jesus' resurrection from the dead (Acts 2:25-32). Peter was convinced of the bodily resurrection of Jesus.

It has been said that to remove the physical resurrection of Jesus Christ from the NT would be to leave huge, gaping holes in the text.

THE TEACHINGS OF CHRIST BEGAN TO CIRCULATE ORALLY

After Christ's ascension, the apostles circulated the message by word of mouth.

Luke records the first instance of spreading the teaching of Jesus in Acts 2:14-36, where Peter gives the first Christian sermon on the day of Pentecost. Luke further records that the first church in Jerusalem was committed to what the witnesses conveyed about Jesus' life and teachings: "They were continually devoting themselves to the apostles' teaching . . ." (Acts 2:42). The gospel quickly spread throughout Jerusalem (Acts 6:7), and from there it disseminated to outlying areas (Acts 8:4), including Samaria (Acts 8:5). Wildfire might be an apt comparison, for the message spread relatively quickly into Gentile regions (Acts chapters 13-14).

The apostle Paul was authorized by the Lord to spread the Word among the Gentiles.

Paul was not one of the original Twelve; neither did he qualify as a witness from the time of the baptism of Christ (see Acts 1:21-23). Nonetheless, the resurrected Jesus charged Paul to bring the gospel message to the Gentiles, and his resulting letters carry that authority.

> "Paul, an apostle (not sent from men nor through the agency of man, but through Jesus Christ and God the Father)." (Gal. 1:1)

> "For I would have you know, brethren, that the gospel which was preached by me is not according to man. For I neither received it from man, nor was I taught it, but I received it through a revelation of Jesus Christ." (Gal. 1:11-12, compare with Acts 9, Paul's conversion account.)[187]

The other apostles recognized Paul's apostleship:

> "But on the contrary, seeing that I had been entrusted with the gospel to the uncircumcised, just as Peter had been to the circumcised (for He who effectually worked for Peter in his apostleship to the circumcised effectually worked for me also to the Gentiles), and recognizing the grace that had been given to me, James and Cephas and John, who were reputed to be pillars, gave to me and Barnabas the right hand of fellowship, so that we might go to the Gentiles and they to the circumcised." (Gal. 2:7-9)

Peter treated Paul's writings on the same level as recognized "Scriptures":

> ". . . our beloved brother Paul, according to the wisdom given him, wrote to you, as also in all his letters, speaking in them of these things, in which are some things hard to understand, which the untaught and unstable distort, as they do also the rest of the Scriptures, to their own destruction." (2 Peter 3:15-16)

Apostolic authority carried great weight with subsequent generations of Christians because of the unique status of the apostles as our Lord's appointed ambassadors. In fact (as we have seen) their authority was so significant and unique that the acceptance of a writing by the early Christians into the Canon depended on the relationship of that writing to the apostles and their teachings.

> **Apostolic authority carried great weight because of the unique status of the apostles as our Lord's appointed ambassadors.**

It is worth noting that by the time of 2 Corinthians 3:14, Paul was referring to the Jewish Scriptures as "the old covenant," implying that the new covenant had surpassed the old.[188] This corresponds to the "new covenant in my blood" of which Jesus spoke during the Last Supper.

The writer of Hebrews clearly asserts that God, who although in the past had communicated to people through the prophets,

> ". . . in these last days has spoken to us in His Son, whom He appointed heir of all things, through whom also He made the world." (Heb. 1:2)

Clearly there was a growing corpus of apostolic teaching that a new revelation from God had now come, and it was inexorably linked to Jesus Christ.

Additionally, the transmission of Jesus' teachings through the apostles was accompanied by validating miraculous signs. The writer of Hebrews captures the sequence of events this way:

> "After it [i.e. the word that offered salvation] was at the first spoken through the Lord, it was confirmed to us by those who heard, God also testifying with them, both by signs and wonders and by

various miracles and by gifts of the Holy Spirit according to His own will." (Heb. 2:3b-4)

IN TIME, THE NEED FOR BROADER CIRCULATION AND AUTHORITATIVE VERSIONS OF THE EVENTS AND TEACHINGS OF CHRIST BECAME EVIDENT

The gospel accounts

Various snippets, called by scholars "the sayings of Jesus," circulated and were of particular value where the apostles were not present. As mentioned in an earlier chapter, many believe that some of these snippets were collected into a document called "Q." Mark probably wrote his account of the gospel sometime late AD 50s to 60s, relying primarily on the teachings of Peter. Matthew and Luke probably became aware of these through travelers or personal meetings.

> Various snippets, called by scholars "the sayings of Jesus," circulated and were of particular value where the apostles were not present.

Matthew (shortly before AD 70) and Luke (mid to late 60s) followed with their biographies using resources which included Mark's account and possibly "Q." Matthew, of course, relied on his own recollections as well. Luke, although not an eyewitness, was a careful historian; he did meticulous research using a wide variety of resources. Finally, John wrote his gospel (AD 80-85), apparently at the urging of others.

By the 2nd century the four gospels accounts were being circulated as the fourfold gospel.

Paul's writings

Paul's thirteen letters were composed between AD 46 and 67. His individual letters began to circulate immediately after he wrote them. In Colossians 4:16, for example, he requested his letter be sent to the Laodiceans and the letter to the Laodiceans (which we do not have) be sent to Colossae. Another example is when Paul wrote a single letter to multiple churches in the Galatia region (Gal. 1:2), which of course would have been circulated either in its original autograph or in copy form.

A collection of Paul's writings became widely known (as evidenced in 1 Peter 3:15-16) which was written to Christians in a wide geographic area (1 Peter 1:1). The extra-biblical record shows that Paul's letters as a collection were in wide circulation by the beginning of the 2nd century. Possibly Timothy or Luke was responsible for gathering Paul's writings into one collection, but this is only conjecture. We simply do not know.

Chronology of the New Testament Documents

Year	Book
48	Galatians
50?	James
52	1 Thessalonians
57-59	Gospel According to Mark
52-53	2 Thessalonians
55	1 & 2 Corinthians
53-57	Romans
60	Colossians, Philemon
60-61	Gospel According to Luke
60-62	Acts
60-66	Gospel According to Matthew
61	Ephesians
61-62	Philippians
62-64	1 Peter
63	1 Timothy, Titus
66-67	2 Timothy
67	2 Peter
67-70	Jude
68-69	Hebrews
90-95	1, 2, 3 John
90-100	Gospel According to John
95-96	Revelation

> Paul's letters as a collection were in wide circulation by the beginning of the 2nd century.

Some of Paul's letters, for reasons unknown, were not included in this collection (see, for example, 1 Corinthians 5:9 and Colossians 4:16). Forgeries of Paul apparently began to circulate during his lifetime. So he warns the Thessalonian believers "not to be quickly shaken in mind or alarmed, either by a spirit or a spoken word, or a letter seeming to be from us, to the effect that the day of the Lord has come." (2 Thess. 2:2)

Other NT writings

James, Peter, Jude, and John wrote letters of instructions to various churches and individuals. These spanned the second half of the 1st century. An anonymous writer penned the book of Hebrews. Finally John wrote his Apocalypse, most likely in the last decade of the 1st century.

PERVERSION OF THE TRUTH WAS ANTICIPATED

The apostles were concerned about potential corruption of their teachings. Paul warned the elders of the church at Ephesus:

> "Be on guard for yourselves and for all the flock, among which the Holy Spirit has made you overseers, to shepherd the church of God which He purchased with His own blood. I know that after my departure savage wolves will come in among you, not sparing the flock; and from among your own selves men will arise, speaking perverse things, to draw away the disciples after them." (Acts 20:28-30)

Peter wrote:

> "But false prophets also arose among the people, just as there will also be false teachers among you, who will secretly introduce destructive heresies, even denying the Master who bought them, bringing swift destruction upon themselves. Many will follow their sensuality, and because of them the way of the truth will be maligned; and in their greed they will exploit you with false words; their judgment from long ago is not idle, and their destruction is not asleep." (2 Peter 2:1-3)

The apostles therefore made provisions for their teachings to be faithfully preserved and circulated. These provisions included the rationale for writing in the first place, but also for the teaching ministry to carry on these truths of the faith. The obvious concern of the apostles was to propagate and preserve the true Christian teachings.

> "Therefore many other signs Jesus also performed in the presence of the disciples, which are not written in this book; but these have been written so that you may believe that Jesus is the Christ, the Son of God; and that believing you may have life in His name." (John 20:30-31)

"The things which you [Timothy] have heard from me [Paul] in the presence of many witnesses, entrust these to faithful men who will be able to teach others also." (2 Tim. 2:2)

Following the Deaths of the Apostles

By the end of the 1st century and beginning of the 2nd, the four accounts of the gospel were in circulation and well-recognized as a fixed group of four biographies of Jesus Christ. Likewise, the writings of Paul and Hebrews were being circulated as a single collection and accepted as authoritative. The other NT writings were in circulation, some of which took longer to be recognized as universally authoritative, due possibly to their brevity or lateness of composition.

True to the apostles' predictions, false teachings and writings surfaced, causing the believers to wrestle with identifying the genuine and rejecting the false. However, by the 4th century, the Canon of twenty-seven books came to be universally accepted as authoritative and inspired by God; and all other books were rejected as non-apostolic or non-authoritative.

The Canon Is Now Closed

> From the time of the 4th century, the Canon has been a complete unit of accepted books, acknowledged by all.

There is today a resurgence of debate concerning the Canon that becomes quite complex and technical. This is significant, because if the Canon is still open, then possibly there are additional written communications from God to us that we are missing. Additionally, some of the NT books may be dismissed as non-authoritative. However, the criteria for acceptance into the Canon are no longer capable of being fulfilled, particularly that of determining apostolic authority. As one scholar has said, "We are 2,000 years too late to make this determination."[189]

From the time of the 4th century, the Canon has been a complete unit of accepted books, acknowledged by all. Neither the debates of the 16th century during the time of the Reformation nor the debates of the present alter what the early Christians accepted as normative and authoritative.

We can safely conclude, therefore, that the NT Canon is closed and is composed of the twenty-seven books identified in our Bibles today.[190]

CHAPTER THIRTEEN

WHAT DIFFERENCE DOES IT MAKE?

We can be confident that the twenty-seven books of the New Testament we have it in our hands today are the writings God intended to be authoritative for us in matters of doctrine and spiritual life. Other ancient books, while possibly having some devotional and historical value, are rightly excluded from the place of inspired, canonical writings.

OUR FAITH IS GROUNDED ON HISTORICAL FACTS

The Christian faith is dependent upon the veracity of the historical facts. If the NT Scriptures are not what they appear to be, then our trust in God, their Author, is unfounded and our hope for the future is not the confident expectation to which the Scriptures testify. However, the NT documents *are* historically reliable—as well as being inspired by God the Holy Spirit—so they form a solid foundation for all we believe.

Most Christians, however, come to faith in the true God of the universe without knowing a great deal about how the Bible came to us. However, when confronted with the liberal bias of the universities and the popular media, doubt can creep in. After all, almost all of what we know about God in an objective and specific sense comes through the Word of God, the Bible, itself. True, we see God's "eternal power and divine nature" in nature in a general way (Rom. 1:20), but the Bible presents God in a more specific, detailed way. And it reveals the great Christian truths related to redemption from sin that Jesus Christ effected at the cross. Without the NT, it would be impossible to know about God's love and grace.

To be sure, the Holy Spirit does play a major role in convincing people that the Bible is the unique Word of God. But how can we be sure that our "conviction" about the truth of the Bible is any different than the "conviction" others may have about, say, the Book of Mormon, or the Qur'an, or for that matter, the Apocrypha? Therefore, this study of the Canon of the New Testament Scriptures is essential for confidence in Christian faith.

We pray that you as the reader will gain more objective and assured confidence in the NT. Despite the constant assaults on its integrity, you can be confident that the NT is the powerful, unalterable Word of God. The entire NT is indeed Scripture in the same way Peter spoke of Paul's writings (2 Peter 3:16). And you can be assured of its value today:

> "All Scripture is inspired by God and profitable for teaching, for reproof, for correction, for training in righteousness." (2 Tim. 3:16)

> Despite the constant assaults on its integrity, you can be confident that the New Testament is the powerful, unalterable Word of God.

Defending the Bible

The first step in defending the Bible is to be confident yourself that it is the Word of God. Faith comes at various levels, depending on each person's need. For some, the need is for discovering the Bible's relevancy. They need to discover its transforming power as they are confronted with it directly. There is truth to the old adage that you don't need to defend a lion, you just need to turn it loose. This can happen when you simply give a gift of the Bible to someone and encourage him or her to begin reading, say, in John's account of the gospel. Or it can happen when you invite someone to read the Bible with you and discuss it. My life was profoundly changed when someone gave me a New Testament with the challenge to read it for myself.

For still others, intellectual barriers have been erected, and false notions about the Bible may run deep. You can help by discovering what questions they have about the history of the Bible and from there helping them understand just how credible the Bible really is. Many people are completely unaware of what you now know. It is for this last group of people that this study is most important.

Finally, you can pass this book on to someone else or point them to some of the resources in the bibliography.

The attacks against the credibility of the Bible will continue. You will probably not find yourself in debates with the liberal scholars of our day, but there are many average people who have been captured by their ideas. The people who accept the erroneous views of the Bible are not the enemy; they have been blinded. Your patience and persistence can make an eternal difference in freeing them from the darkness of unbelief. Ultimately, the greatest demonstration of the credibility of the Bible is the credibility of those who believe the Bible is the Word of God, whose lives have been remarkably changed through the Christ of Scripture. By allowing God's Word (the written Word and the living Word) to live in and through you, you become walking proof that the Bible is powerful, relevant, and life-changing in our day.

So, turn the Bible loose and see what God can do with His Word!

Chapter Fourteen

Conclusion

The brief outline presented in this book[191] has demonstrated that there is credible historical evidence for the integrity of the NT Canon. While no historical research can bring absolute certitude in and of itself, we can be as sure of the Canon as we can of any other historical document—in fact, more sure! And we can be confident that the events and teachings communicated in the NT are true to what really happened and what was really taught by the Lord Jesus Christ and His apostles.

Our fellow Christians of the early church era, who were much closer in time to Jesus and the apostles, have performed an immeasurable service in identifying and preserving the apostolic writings. And we praise God for using them to fulfill what Jesus prophesied: "Heaven and earth will pass away, but My words will not pass away." (Luke 21:33)

By faith we take the credibility of this history and go the next step. We do not want to be like those who had the revelation of God but rebelled:

> "For indeed we have had good news preached to us, just as they also; but the word they heard did not profit them, because it was not united by faith in those who heard." (Heb. 4:2)

We are blessed to have the written Word of God handed down to us so that we might read, study, and live by the truths God presents in it. We are called on to embrace it by faith. "Faith comes from hearing, and hearing by the word of Christ." (Rom. 10:17)

POSTSCRIPT: FAITH & HISTORY

There is a reciprocal relationship between truth and faith. What one sees as true affects what one believes. Conversely, what a person believes affects how he sees the truth. None of us humans can be completely objective, and this includes historians and theologians. This being a stark and sobering thing to realize for oneself, I too am affected by subjective influences. However, it is far better to acknowledge human limitations than to pretend perfect objectivity or presume all knowledge and insight. With that in mind, I present here simply what I believe to be truth.

> The *belief* that the contents of the New Testament documents are *not* inspired can taint one's perception of the historical processes.

With great effort I have tried to handle the historical data objectively, but I admit that I do approach the material by faith as well. Even those who reject the integrity of the NT documents approach the subject with a certain amount of faith and presumption, for non-belief can indeed be a form of belief. The *belief* that the contents of the NT documents are *not* inspired can taint one's perception of the historical processes. Second, there is much dependence on conjecture and probabilities, plus reliance on previous scholars and writers who also appeal to much conjecture and probabilities. This dependence is so prevalent that one could hardly deny a certain amount of faith is involved in trusting the research of others, if not faith in the integrity of what others have concluded and written. Post-modern thinking is no exception in that it requires faith in one's own ability to think and rationalize correctly. There is also a belief that it is impossible to know anything with certainty, even historical events. So we must conclude that all are affected by their beliefs without exception.

In the end, the reader is left to evaluate for him or herself what has been presented herein and to take a stand for what they believe to be the true understanding of the historical facts concerning the Canon of the NT writings.

I have presented this material for two reasons. Though raised in a religious home, skepticism had enveloped my college years concerning the existence of God and the contents of the Bible. After completing my undergraduate training in Mathematics at Oregon State University in 1972, I moved to western New York, where like many college graduates I was skeptical of all things religious. However, finding myself confronted by other young adults who had a vibrant faith in Jesus Christ and a devotion to reading the Bible, I was perplexed. Their lives seemed whole and complete; mine was anything but that. Yet I debated them at every level, trying to prove that faith in Jesus Christ was misguided and a thing of a by-gone age. I assaulted them with my best arguments, being the classic skeptic as I was.

Then one of them presented me with a New Testament in modern English and challenged me to read it and evaluate it for myself. My heart began to "burn" within me as I found the Word of God speaking deeply to my soul. Realizing that I was separated from the One who had created me, I was nevertheless overwhelmed by a love so compelling, so wonderful, a love demonstrated on a cross 2,000 years ago, a love that could free me from a life of purposelessness, selfishness, and rebellion against God. In a driveway of a small house in western New York I repented of my rebellion against my Maker and turned to Him for salvation, believing that Jesus Christ died in my place, for my sins. My tenacious skepticism gave way to a tenacious faith. It has now been over thirty-seven years since that time, twenty-seven of those in fulltime service for the Lord. A "healthy" skepticism has continued to drive me to "test all things" as to whether they be true or not—in order to arrive at a level of certitude on which I can continue to build my faith.

My confidence in the historical integrity of the NT Scriptures, together with an unshakeable faith in the God of history, leads me to clearly and unashamedly affirm . . .

... that the NT (along with the OT) is God's communication to us today.

... that God inspired faithful eyewitnesses to record narratives of the life and teachings of Jesus Christ and that He inspired various other writers to apply God's revelation to specific circumstances for the edification of the church through the ages and to put those teachings into written form.

... that God providentially guided the subsequent generations of Christians in recognizing those writings as authoritative and preserving them for the benefit of future generations of Christians.

... that the Bibles we have in our hands, though the translations may differ, include the writings God intends to be authoritative for us today, and therefore we can be confident that they reflect God's mind for us.

... that showing the NT documents are credible is not absolute proof that they are from God. The final proof lies in the results of our faith when we believe the Bible to be the Word of God.

... that faith (trust) in the teachings of the Bible is necessary to move this study from being merely academic to living out of the truth in our lives:

> "But one who looks intently at the perfect law, the law of liberty, and abides by it, not having become a forgetful hearer but an effectual doer, this man will be blessed in what he does." (James 1:25)

GLOSSARY

Apocrypha – Refers to writings included in the Septuagint, Orthodox and Roman Catholic Bibles but not in the Jewish Bible or most contemporary Protestant Bibles. Members of the groups that accept these books as canonical tend to call them the "deutero-canonical" books.

Apostolic Fathers – Writers in the era that immediately followed the time of the apostles some of whom had personal acquaintance with them. These generally date from the end of the 1st century AD into the first half of the 2nd century.

Autographs – The original documents of the Bible as actually penned by the writers. Today, we only have copied manuscripts.

Canon – A fixed list of books or letters determined to be authoritative in a particular community. In the Christian community, it refers to the 27 recognized books of the NT and the 39 books of the OT.

Church Fathers – Early Christian writers (including the apostolic fathers). These date from roughly the 2nd centuries through the time of the Nicene Council (AD 325).

Codex – A bound book made up of folded leaves or pages. Codices gradually replaced scrolls as the medium for written transmission of the Bible and other ancient texts.

Council of Nicaea – Convened in AD 325, this was the first time after the apostles that churches leaders representing all the churches of Christendom gathered to settle doctrinal disputes.

Deutero-canonical – Refers to books beyond the twenty-seven canonical books of the NT, generally called the Apocrypha by Protestants. This term (deutero-canonical) is used by those who hold the Apocrypha in high regard, such as the Roman Catholic and Orthodox churches.

Epistle – A transliteration of the Greek word for "a written letter."

Eusebius – An early church historian, who preserved much of the writings of the apostolic fathers and other early church fathers. Without his work of preservation, we would know little of the early Christian activities and teachings.

Extant – In reference to ancient manuscripts, this means a document exists today. For example we have an extant fragmentary copy of a portion of The Gospel According to John from the 2nd century AD—a person today could go to Manchester, England and actually see it. The earliest extant complete copy of the NT is the Codex Sinaiticus which dates from the 4th century.

Gnosticism – A religious and philosophical movement from about the 1st century BC through the 3rd century CE. Its name comes from the Greek word *gnosis*, which means "knowledge." Gnosticism claimed secret knowledge that ensured salvation.

Jesus Seminar – A modern effort to capture what some scholars think were the original and authentic words of Jesus. Using suspect criteria, they dismiss much of the NT gospel's record of Jesus teachings.

Manuscript – Abbreviated as MSS, this term usually refers to subsequent hand-written copies of the original documents of the NT documents and related writings.

MSS – An abbreviation of "manuscript."

Nag Hammadi – The location in Egypt where a cache of ancient documents was found in 1945, which included the so-called Gnostic texts that date from the 4th century.

NT – Abbreviation for New Testament.

Oral tradition – Before the gospel was circulated in written form, the teachings of Christ were passed around by word of mouth. The early Christians relied greatly on the oral transmission of the apostles' teachings about Christ.

Orthodox – "Conforming to traditional or generally accepted beliefs." In the context of church history, while these is a universally accepted basic core of beliefs, there is much debate among the various "Christian" traditions about certain teachings, such as justification, the nature of the church, etc.

Orthodox Church – Variously used to refer to the division in Christianity between the Roman Catholic (or western) church and the Orthodox (eastern) church, which brewed over the centuries and finally brought division around 900 years after Christ. Various traditions trace their history back to this division, identified with regions or countries (e.g. Eastern Orthodox, Greek Orthodox, Russian Orthodox, etc.)

OT – Abbreviation for Old Testament.

Papyrus – A type of ancient writing material made from an aquatic plant, primarily found in Egypt.

Polemic – The practice of disputing or controverting religious, philosophical, or political matters. As such, a polemical text on a topic is often written specifically to dispute or refute a position or doctrine.

Pseudepigraphy – This term is generally applied to those writings which are distinctly spurious, falsely claiming to have been written by biblical authors.

Reformation – Referring to the time period beginning in the early 1500s AD, the start of which is traditionally identified with Martin Luther, a German monk who challenged the Roman Catholic Church on the subject of justification and the selling of indulgences. The original intent was to reform the church, but the actions of Luther and others led to a schism resulting in a movement called Protestantism.

Sayings of Jesus – A way of referring to the oral transmission of the teaching of Christ before the written gospels were in full circulation.

Septuagint – A Greek translation of the Hebrew Bible completed 2nd century BC. Later versions of it, by the 4th century AD, included the Apocrypha.

Vellum – A type of ancient writing material made of animal skins.

Vulgate – A translation of the Bible into Latin, traditionally ascribed to Jerome (c.a. 347-420) and which held sway in the western church for close to 1,000 years.

ANNOTATED BIBLIOGRAPHY

Bock, Darrell L. *Jesus According to Scripture: Restoring the Portrait from the Gospels.* Grand Rapids: Baker Book House, 2002.

Bock, Darrell L., and Daniel B. Wallace. *Dethroning Jesus: Exposing Popular Culture's Quest to Unseat the Biblical Christ.* Nashville: Thomas Nelson, 2007.

Bruce, F. F. *The Canon of Scripture.* Downers Grove, IL: InterVarsity Press, 1988. An excellent treatment of how the Old and NT came into being.

Bruce, F. F. *The New Testament Documents: Are They Reliable?* Downers Grove, IL: InterVarsity Press, 1981. This classic, first published in 1943, has been updated and reprinted over and over again. It remains one of the most popular introductions to this subject.

Carson, D. A., and Douglas J. Moo. *An Introduction to the New Testament.* Grand Rapids: Zondervan, 2005. A comprehensive overview and well argued presentation of canonical matters, for both the whole NT as well as the individual books.

Carson, D. A., and John D. Woodbridge, eds. *Hermeneutics, Authority and Canon.* Eugene, OR: Wipf & Stock Publishers, 2005. This is a collection of papers presented that address contemporary issues concerning the relationship between Hermeneutics, Authority and the Canon, just as the title suggests.

Geisler, Norman L., and William E. Nix. *A General Introduction to the Bible.* Chicago: Moody Press, 1979. This is a broad treatment of the subject of how the Bible came into being, was collected, transmitted and translated so that we have the Bible in our language and in our hands today.

Lightfoot, J. B. *The Apostolic Fathers.* Grand Rapids: Baker Book House, 1978. Contains the complete texts of the "Apostolic Fathers."

Metzger, Bruce M. *The Canon of the New Testament.* Oxford: Clarendon Press, 1997. An excellent resource by one of most widely recognized authorities on the textual development of the Bible.

Wegner, Paul D. *The Journey from Text to Translations: The Origin and Development of the Bible.* Ada, MI: Baker Book House, 1999. The title accurately reflects the content of the book. This is a comprehensive work that brings together much information in an easy to read format.

Online resources supporting the reliability of the four gospels.

The Center for Study of New Testament Manuscripts (www.csntm.org). Founded by Daniel B. Wallace (Executive Director). A primary purpose of this organization is to "To make digital photographs of extant Greek New Testament manuscripts so that such images can be preserved, duplicated without deterioration, and accessed by scholars doing textual research." You can find online thousands of pages of high definition photographs of ancient manuscripts.

www.apologetics.com. Features a variety of solid apologetic resources, including several related to the gospels. Check the "Articles" link.

www.apologeticsindex.org. Indexes a vast number of apologetics websites of varying worth. Using the index on the home page, one can look for specific articles. See "Jesus," for example.

www.benwitherington.blogspot.com. Includes writings on many topics by a top New Testament scholar. Often rebuts current attacks on Jesus and the canonical gospels (for example, an excellent series on the supposed tomb of Jesus). Lacks an index, so use the "Search Blog" function at the top.

www.bible.org. One of the top Bible websites. The Bibliology section (under "Theology: Articles and Studies") has ample resources for Bible study, including some fine pieces on Canon and textual criticism.

www.codexsinaiticus.org. Presents a complete set of high definition photographs fo the entire Codex Sinaiticus, the earliest complete NT manuscript.

www.comparative-religion.com/christianity/apocrypha/. This online collection includes an exhaustive compilation of all apocryphal books of the early Church times.

www.earlychristianwritings.com. This is an excellent compilation of most of the early Christian writings.

www.leestrobel.com. Features apologetic video clips. "Investigating Jesus" section includes helpful materials on the canonical gospels.

www.probe.org. Filled with apologetics resources. Check the "Reasons to Believe" section for well-researched articles on the gospels, or use the search function with "gospels."

www.themoorings.org. An apologetics site run by Ed Rickard. While not flinching from taking controversial doctrinal positions, this site offers well-researched sections devoted to the reliability of the canonical gospels accounts.

The following are a sampling of resources for studying those who question the credibility of the NT in one degree or another.

Ehrman, Bart. *Misquoting Jesus: The Story of Who Changed the Bible and Why.* New York: Harper Collins, 2005. Ehrman is a leading voice who attempts to discredit the reliability of the NT documents.

Gamble, Harry Y. *The New Testament Canon: Its Making and Meaning.* Eugene, OR: Wipf & Stock Publishers, 2002.

Hahneman, Geoffrey Mark. *The Muratorian Fragment and the Development of the Canon.* Oxford: Oxford University Press, 1992.

McDonald, Lee Martin, and James A. Sanders, eds. *The Canon Debate.* Peabody, MA: Hendrickson Publishers, 2002.

McDonald, Lee Martin. *The Formation of the Christian Biblical Canon: Revised and Expanded Edition.* Peabody, MA: Hendrickson Publishers, 1995.

Pagels, Elaine. *The Gnostic Gospels.* New York: Random House, 1989.

von Campenhausen, Hans. *The Fathers of the Church.* Peabody, MA: Hendrickson Publishers, 1998.

von Campenhausen, Hans. *The Formation of the Christian Bible.* Philadelphia: Fortress, 1972.

www.westarinstitute.org/index.html. The Westar Institute is the home of the well-known "Jesus Seminar," whose designed intention is to judge the relative credibility of the NT Gospels. A collection of scholars gathers twice yearly to debate the relative authenticity of Jesus' words and then vote with colored beads to gather a consensus on what Jesus said. Other seminars sponsored by Westar include: The Paul Seminar, the Canon Seminar, and the Acts Seminar.

Endnotes

Chapter 1
Introduction to the Issue

[1] Quoted in David G. Dunbar, "The Biblical Canon," chapter 9, in *Hermeneutics, Authority and Canon*, by D. A. Carson and John D. Woodbridge, eds. (Eugene, OR: Wipf & Stock Publishers, 2005), 300.

[2] Harry Y. Gamble, *The New Testament Canon* (Philadelphia: Fortress Press, 1985), 13. He goes on to explain that this is due to modern discoveries of early Christian literature of which little has been known about before or knew about second handedly. Ecumenical discussions have brought to light the differing perceptions of what the Canon is and how it came to be among various branches of Christendom. Yet, as we will see below, much of the "new" discoveries, have been seen reflected in the writings of the early Christian writes as they debated and defended against aberrant views.

[3] "Reflections on Jesus and the New Testament Canon," in *The Canon Debate*, by Lee Martin McDonald and James A. Sanders, ed. (Peabody, MA: Hendrickson, 2002), 19.

[4] See for example, Robert W. Funk, *A Credible Jesus: Fragments of a Vision* (Santa Rosa: Polebridge, 2002).

[5] Gamble, 84. Protestant scholars look within scripture for the overriding interpretative principle, whereas Catholic scholars look externally, to the church authority (see Gamble, 82).

[6] D. A. Carson and Douglas J. Moo, *An Introduction to the New Testament* (Grand Rapids, MA: Zondervan, 2005), 727.

7 David G. Dunbar, "The Biblical Canon," chapter 9, in *Hermeneutics, Authority and Canon*, D. A. Carson and John D. Woodbridge, eds. (Eugene, OR: Wipf & Stock Publishers, 2005), 318.

8 *Easton's Bible Dictionary*, s.v. "canon." In fact, the word in the Greek is used in Galatians 6:16 to mean "rule."

9 Carson and Moo, 726. The earliest known use of the term Canon in this latter connection is furnished by Athanasius around AD 350 (see Gamble, 17).

10 Quoted in Bruce M. Metzger, *The Canon of The New Testament: Its Origin, Development, and Significance* (Oxford: Oxford University Press, 1987), 13.

11 See, for example, the website of the Greek Orthodox Archdiocese of America, www.goarch.org/en/ourfaith/articles/article8032.asp for a further explanation.

12 Gamble, 19.

Chapter 2
The Need for Credibility

13 Some modern scholars want to conjecture and turn all the evidence in the most advantageous light to support things which would otherwise strain credibility. One begins to question the objectivity of such scholars who slant the historical details with the over abundance of words like "possible" and "probable." The question is which interpretation presents a more credible explanation of the historical facts.

14 True, this warning applies specifically to the Book of the Revelation, but it provides an example of how the writers emphasize the importance of what they have written.

15 Sir William Ramsey, quoted in F. F. Bruce, *The New Testament Documents: Are They Reliable?* 6th ed. (Grand Rapids: Eerdmans, 1981), 91-92. Ramsey devoted many years to archaeology of Asia Minor. When he first set out, he was "firmly convinced of the truth . . . that Acts was a late production of the middle of the 2nd century AD, and was only gradually compelled to a complete reversal of his views by the inescapable evidence of the facts uncovered in the course of his research." Bruce goes on to say that research into historical and geographical backgrounds of the NT has continued on since the time of Ramsey, "but our respect for Luke's reliability continues to grow as our knowledge of this field increases."

16 Dunbar, 318-21.

17 Dunbar, 320.

[18] Quoted in Dunbar, 321.

[19] Bauer in fact asserts that the original manifestation of Christianity was one that would later be judged heretical by the orthodox. Of course, this is highly speculative with no clear foundation in historical fact. See Dunbar, 321.

Chapter 3
An Historical Overview of the Resources

[20] Gamble, 57-68.

[21] See also Hebrews 2:4.

[22] Even such modern media resource would not be of much more help because of the well-known capability for "doctoring" even audio signals and digital imaging.

[23] Carson and Moo, 31. Of course, it could be countered that virtually all of the original writings of classic and Greek literature have disappeared. But, for people of faith, the explanation is plausible.

[24] Letterpress printing was not invented until the mid-15th century, with the first Greek New Testament printed in 1514 (Carson and Moo, 26). For a modern day attempt to duplicate the work of scribes see *www.saintjohnsbible.org*.

[25] Dr. Daniel Wallace of *The Center for the Study of New Testament Manuscripts* (*www.csntm.org*) is leading an effort to create high definition digital photos of manuscripts and make them available to the general public. This effort, in effect frees the manuscripts from the confines of museums and monasteries for viewing by scholars and researchers, as well as the general public.

[26] This manuscript in its entirety has been reproduced in digital form by an international collaboration to reunite the document and make it accessible to a global audience. "Drawing on the expertise of leading scholars, conservators and curators, the Project gives everyone the opportunity to connect directly with this famous manuscript." The results are posted on the internet at *www.codexsinaiticus.org* and as of July 6, 2009, all extant pages of the codex are included.

[27] Although the evidence is that the Codex Vaticanus originally included the entire NT, certain pages of the extant MSS are missing which contain the last portion of Hebrews, 1 and 2 Timothy, Titus, Philemon and Revelation. This was apparently due to damage to the back of the volume. Likewise, the book of Genesis is missing because of apparent damage to the front of the volume. Such damage is not uncommon among ancient manuscripts, due to use over time.

[28] Elwell, W. A., and Beitzel, B. J. *Baker Encyclopedia of the Bible* (Grand Rapids: Baker Book House, 1997), 315. See also, Carson and Moo, 26.

[29] David G. Dunbar, "The Biblical Canon," chapter 9, in *Hermeneutics, Authority and Canon*, D. A. Carson and John D. Woodbridge, eds. (Eugene, OR: Wipf & Stock Publishers, 2005), 316.

[30] It should be noted that the church Fathers quoted from and referenced other books besides the ones which eventually were included in the Canon. Thus, the mere fact that a document was quoted by an early writer does not mean it automatically should be considered canonical. Both the context and the intention of the writer need to be considered.

Chapter 4
Apostolic Authority of the Gospel

[31] F. F. Bruce, *The Canon of Scripture* (Downers Grove, IL: InterVarsity Press, 1988), 119-20.

[32] Gamble, 24-25.

[33] Carson and Moo, 85.

[34] Papias, Oracles, 1.

[35] Gamble, 26-27.

[36] Carson and Moo, 739.

[37] Ibid. 24.

[38] Gamble, 27. Gamble might object to calling the Marcionites an "aberrant sect," yet the Marcionites were clearly rejected by the church at large.

[39] 1st Letter of Clement to the Corinthians, 13.

[40] Most scholars now agree that the writing titled "The 2nd letter of Clement to the Corinthians" was probably not written by Clement of Rome, but by another individual.

[41] The word translated "scriptures" can refer to "the writings" and not necessarily "divinely inspired Scripture" in the present day sense. Just the same, it is clear some level of authority is implied by use of the formula "as Scripture says."

[42] Although it is not absolutely certain whether Justin Martyr actually knew of Mark and John's gospel, most recognize by the end of the 2nd century that the Diatessaron points to the existence of the four.

⁴³ Gamble, 28.

⁴⁴ Dunbar, 334.

⁴⁵ Ibid. 30. Gamble in one place claims that Tatian used other sources besides the four gospel accounts, yet seems to contradict himself when he later says, "While Tatian did not rely exclusively on our Gospels, it is not certain that he made extensive use of any other gospel-type document, as has often been supposed."

⁴⁶ Gamble explains that "Irenaeus' torturous defense of the four Gospel accounts indicate that their acceptance was rather new or novel at his time." He says, "If such issues had to be addressed, then the four-fold Gospel collection had not yet become established beyond all objection" (Gamble, 33). This effort of Gamble's seems like an effort at all costs to undermine the obvious. By this reasoning, one could say there has never been any settled acceptance of anything in the church, because one could always find at least one objection! There have always been challenges to the truth at every stage of church history. It is entirely possible and most likely probable, that in the face of growing divergent teaching (that which was contrary to the "traditions" handed down from the apostles), there was need for a renewed apologetic for the authority of the Gospel accounts. Irenaeus defense was simply a refinement back to what was originally held. Gamble has not proved his point.

⁴⁷ Quoted in Dunbar, 334 (taken from *Against Heresies*, 2.28.2).

⁴⁸ Dunbar, 337.

⁴⁹ "The unanimity of the attributions in the 2nd century cannot be explained by anything other than the assumption that the titles were part of the works from the beginning." Carson and Moo, 141.

⁵⁰ Most of what Papias wrote has been lost to antiquity, only fragments have survived. Eusebius later (4th century) questioned Papias' motivation, but nonetheless, Papias is among the very earliest post-apostolic writings.

⁵¹ Oracles, 6. Some scholars dispute whether the Matthew referred to here is the same as the writer of The Gospel According to Matthew. Debating the technical questions such as these are beyond the scope of this writing. I refer the reader to D. A. Carson and Douglas J. Moo, "An Introduction to the New Testament."

⁵² Dating NT documents can be difficult. Conservative scholars determine the approximate dates of a written document by considering several things: 1) the approximate dates of the earliest reference to that document, 2) references inside the document to historical events and 3) specific comments by subsequent writers in the early church (for example Eusebius). Even then, sometimes agreement and certainty are difficult.

53 Papias, as quoted in Eusebius, Hist. Ecc. 3.39.14. Gamble does not give much weight to this quote concerning Mark. However, there is no valid reason for selectively questioning Eusebius' rendition of Papias' writings in this regard, yet relying on Eusebius' history in other areas.

54 Irenaeus, *Against Heresies*, 3.1.1.

55 J. W. Drane, *Introducing the New Testament* (Oxford: Lion Publishing, 2000), 197.

56 In fact, "no dissenting voice from the early church regarding the authorship of the second gospel is found." (Carson and Moo, 174).

57 You can observe Luke's partnership with Paul on his missionary journeys by examining the "we/they" passages in the book of Acts (chapters 16-28).

58 See for, example, in 1 Corinthians 7:10 where he refers to a command from the Lord about marriage and divorce. This was spoken by our Lord during his earthly ministry, which event Paul was not a personal eyewitness to, but had heard about from the other apostles.

59 It is true that Paul may have been referring to a "Q" document or to a "saying of Jesus" that eventually became incorporated into the Gospel of Luke, and not to the Gospel of Luke per se. However, it is clear that he refers to a written source. Since the only extant source we have containing that quote is the Gospel of Luke, the burden of proof lies with those who believe Paul is not referring the Gospel of Luke.

60 Eusebius, *Hist. Eccl.* 5.8.2-4.

61 Had Paul died before the book of Acts was completed it would be difficult to account for the book's silence in regard to so significant an event in this account of his ministry and travels.

62 F. F. Bruce, *The Gospel of John* (Basingstoke, United Kingdom: Pickering & Inglis, 1983), 1.

63 Irenaeus, *Against Heresies*, 3.1.1.

64 Quoted in Carson and Moo, 230.

65 Carson and Moo, 233. Some have suggested that there was an "elder John" distinct from the apostle John, however this is far from certain. Even if there was such a person it is still less obvious that he would have written anything without distinguishing himself from the well-known apostle John. See Carson and Moo, 235.

66 Gamble asserts that John 21 was not written by the same author as John 1-20. However, he admits that there are no manuscripts which exclude John 21 (see Gamble, 28).

⁶⁷ "If such a document existed and was thought of so highly by Matthew and Luke that they quoted extensively from it, why did not the church also regard it highly and preserve it?" John F. Walvoord and Roy B. Zuck, eds., *The Bible Knowledge Commentary: An Exposition of the Scriptures by Dallas Seminary Faculty* (Wheaton, IL: Victor Books, 1983), 14. This view is held by virtually none of the current faculty in the NT department at Dallas Seminary.

⁶⁸ From a spiritual perspective, the similarities can be attributed to the spiritual Author being involved in all three writings, namely the Holy Spirit. However, this is a theological conclusion that is premature to the historical investigation of the evidence.

⁶⁹ Carson and Moo refer to "Q" document theory or "two source theory" that Mark and "Q" were used by Matthew and Luke, as the best working hypothesis, despite the unanswered questions associated with it (103). For a detailed outline and evaluation of the various possible scenarios, see the chapter in Carson and Moo, "The Synoptic Gospels."

⁷⁰ For a list of some of these similarities and identical wordings (see Carson and Moo, 89).

⁷¹ It is notable that Mark had failed in his first recorded attempts at serving the Lord when He abandoned Paul and Barnabas on the first missionary journey (see Acts 13:13) and Paul did not find him useful after that (Acts 15:37-38). Yet, Mark's time with Barnabas and subsequent Christian growth led him to write the story of Christ with the perspective of servanthood. One wonders if his experience influenced the servanthood account of Christ or whether the writing of his account affected his attitude toward serving. At any rate, in the end Paul once again found him useful for service (2 Tim. 4:11).

CHAPTER 5
APOSTOLIC AUTHORITY OF ACTS AND THE LETTERS

⁷² Irenaeus, *Against Heresies*, 3:13.3.

⁷³ In this book, we use "epistle" and "letter" interchangeably.

⁷⁴ Scholars differ on the dates, but these are probably the outside parameters of acceptable dates by conservative scholars. See Bruce, Paul, *Apostle of the Heart Set Free*, 475, Carson and Moo, 335.

⁷⁵ Indeed, Paul said, ". . . and last of all, as to one untimely born, He appeared to me also." However, it is clear that this appearance to Paul (first recorded in Acts 9) was of a different nature (shining light, loud voice, violent reaction of the people nearby) than that given to the other disciples.

76 These same arguments could be leveled against other theories: a) Paul's letters were read, and then laid aside until a time after Acts was written, b) An individual collected Paul's writings in the 2nd century to combat Gnostic thinking, reworking smaller segments into seven or so letters, c) A "Pauline school" of his followers assumed responsibility for the continuation of Paul's work after his death, with not just preserving some of Paul's writings, but in some cases extensively editing of his writings. All these theories make grand assumptions and inferences. But, there is virtually no manuscript evidence to support them. Paul's writings come down to us intact. It is far simpler and more probably that Paul in fact wrote his letters, they were circulated widely and someone at some point simply collected them into a grouping and further circulated them as a corpus of Paul's teaching.

77 See *1st Epistle of Clement to the Corinthians*, 47:1.

78 Carson and Moo, 732.

79 Ibid. 344.

80 Some scholars today date the Muratorian Canon into the 3rd or 4th centuries. However, Everett Ferbuson in 1982 refuted this notion. See Dunbar, 339.

81 Bruce, *The Canon of Scripture*, 130.

82 A codex was an early book form, utilizing leaflets fixed together in a book like form. This was an innovation that quickly rivaled the scroll as the primarily medium for writing literature (see below).

83 The other two James's in the NT were fairly obscure. The early church writers differed between the more well known individuals, James the apostle and James the half-brother of Jesus.

84 Carson and Moo, 631, 738.

85 Ibid. 728.

86 Carson and Moo, 671.

87 In fact, the majority of modern scholars overwhelmingly reject the evidence in favor of a "Johannine school" that "prematurely ruled out" the genuine authorship of John. (Ibid. 674).

88 As mentioned earlier, many scholars today believe the Muratorian Canon is better dated to the 4th century. The debate is still out on this.

89 Often modern liberal scholars counter that books like Revelation were not universally accepted as a means to undermine their authority in the early church. However, because Revelation was not accepted by a the heretic Marcion or the 2nd century group called "The Alogoi," does not take away from the

fact that the book was otherwise well established among most of the churches. There will always be some who reject parts of the consensus of accepted books.

[90] To be sure, there was some dissention in the early church but these were minor. Even Gamble admits that direct witness to Revelation is in Justin Martyr and the book was also cited extensively by Irenaeus (late 2nd century). Tertullian quoted from it and "knew of none but Marcion who did not accept it."

[91] The book of the Revelation was for a time questioned by the Eastern church with some attributing its authorship to forgery by one Cerinthus, a heretic. See Carson and Moo, 734.

[92] Carson and Moo, 601.

[93] Metzger, 159.

[94] See Metzger, 130.

[95] The suggestions include: Barnabas, Clement of Rome, Luke, Apollos.

CHAPTER 6
INFLUENCING THE SPREAD

[96] Many liberal scholars would object to referring to the teachings of various sects as "false" or "unorthodox" for this presupposes that the "orthodox" teachings are right and true. There is a sense in which this objection is valid, in that not everything the early church embraced as orthodox is agreed to by all Bible-believing Christians today. Particularly, the rise of ecclesiastical rank and the movement toward centralized authority has been a central contention for the Protestant movement. The Christian church has at various times in its history had to deal with doctrinal drift or, as some may call it, "doctrinal development." The question for the early church (and for us today) remained, that since the apostles are no longer present, how could Christians determine what was authoritative teaching and what was not? The Roman church in time asserted its primacy as the centralized authority, claiming that the traditional teaching of the Roman Catholic Church is the determination of orthodoxy. Others, this writer included, believe that the determination for evaluating doctrine rests with the inspired writings alone.

[97] The word "tradition" in contemporary conservative circles has fallen onto scorn because it often is used to refer to those churches which follow the "traditions" of man as opposed to the leading of the Spirit and the Scripture. However, in the study of Bibliology, the term simply refers to that which was "passed down," either orally or in written form, without any negative connotations. It is in this sense that Paul uses the term favorably, "Now I praise you because you remember me in everything and hold firmly to the traditions, just as I delivered them to you" (1 Corinthians 11:2).

[98] Carson and Moo, 734.

[99] Many liberal scholars today distinguish between the "orthodox" arm of the church and the various sects and strains which they say were also part of the church. Pagels, for example, considers Gnosticism to have been one of a number of competing factions within the church, but simply having a different perspective on the truth in contrast with the "orthodox" perspective associated with the church Fathers like Irenaeus, Justin Martyr, etc.

[100] Elaine Pagels, *The Gnostic Gospels* (New York: Vintage Books, 1989), 37.

[101] One can see in the Nicene Creed, formulated in the 4th century the clear stand the church took on the issue of the incarnation of Christ: ". . . the Lord Jesus Christ . . . very God of very God, begotten not made . . . being of one substance with the Father . . . who for us men, and for our salvation, came down and was incarnate and was made man . . ."

[102] By orthodox we mean, "Adhering to the accepted or traditional and established faith" (*The American Heritage Dictionary*, s.v. "orthodox").

[103] Bruce, *The Canon of Scripture*, 134.

[104] Metzger, 99. Yet, there are those, like Gamble, who disregard any influence the Marcionite movement had on the formation of the gospel or the speed in which it developed. However, without any admission of contradiction, Gamble admits in the end the collective impact Marcionism, Gnosticism, and Montanism in pressuring the church to be more precise in the source of authoritative written truth. (Gamble, 62). Carson and Moo add, "Undoubtedly the work of Marcion and of other heretics spurred the church to publish more comprehensive and less idiosyncratic lists." (Carson and Moo, 732).

[105] Surprisingly, the church quickly departed from a very simple form of local church government and independence (as described in the NT) and embraced an increasingly hierarchical, institutionalized form of organization.

Chapter 7
The Apostolic Fathers

[106] Some put the date of Clement's letter as early as AD 69.

[107] Dunbar, 323.

[108] Ibid, 324.

[109] Very early in the history of the church, the concept of "bishop" or "elder" migrated from a plurality to a singular, hierarchical position of ecclesiastical authority.

[110] *Epistle of Ignatius to the Philadelphians*, 8.

[111] Metzger, 51.

[112] Bruce, *The Canon of Scripture*, 156.

[113] Metzger, 52.

[114] Ibid, 55.

[115] The author was probably not the Hermas of Romans 16:14.

[116] Simply quoting from another work does not mean that that work was generally accepted as authoritative for all Christians. Indeed, there were numerous books rejected from the Canon that were thought by some at various times to be inspired. However, the reasons for rejection or acceptance was clear (as demonstrated elsewhere in this book).

[117] Dunbar, 340.

[118] C. F. H. Henry, *God, Revelation, and Authority* (Wheaton, IL: Crossway Books, 1999), 4:435-436.

Chapter 8
The Later Church Fathers

[119] Darrell L. Bock, *Breaking the Da Vinci Code* (Nashville, TN: Thomas Nelson, 2004), xvi.

[120] Gamble, speaking for many liberal scholars, says, "The faith of the Christian community . . . had itself been shaped from an early time by many of the same documents which ultimately became canonical. By a fruitful synergy, scripture helped to mold the tradition of faith, and the tradition of faith helped to shape the canon of scripture." Gamble goes on to say that this criterion was never applied to the Synoptic Gospel accounts or Paul's writings. Their orthodoxy was taken for granted since they had been valued for so long and used so widely. Thus, in his opinion, this criterion was used primarily with those writings whose authority was uncertain (Gamble 69).

[121] Disagreement continues to this day about the legitimacy of Roman priority in Christendom. The Roman Catholic Church asserts the doctrine of apostolic succession in which bishops today follow in a long line of succession from the very apostles themselves, with the Pope being the direct successor of the apostle Peter (who in their terms is the "vicar" of Christ). The primacy of the bishop of Rome came to be associated with Peter, and thus came to have controlling authority over all other churches. The Orthodox Church (in its many forms) rejects the primacy of Rome and the papacy. Protestant churches in

general reject the overall concept of apostolic succession including the primacy of Rome (or any other church) and the succession of Peter's apostolate in the papacy. Ironically, in practice denominationalism among many Protestants inherently has assumed a measure of centralized control, though not to the same extent or with the same weight of dogma as does the Roman Catholic Church. In short, where humans are involved, there will always be a tendency for power struggles to control one another's beliefs and practices. This, we believe, is not what Jesus intended when he founded his church upon the rock (Greek: petra meaning massive rock, ridge, shelf of rock) of faith, as expressed by Peter (Greek: petros meaning stone) (Matt 16:18). Peter was not the "Rock" on which the church is built. Rather, the word play would lead us to see him as a stone, who represented the faith of the church. And it is this faith (the principle of faith, not Peter's specific instance of faith) that is the Rock on which the church is built. See Liddell, H. (1996). A Lexicon: Abridged from Liddell and Scott's Greek-English Lexicon. Oak Harbor, WA: Logos Research Systems, Inc., A Greek-English Lexicon of the New Testament and Other Early Christian Literature, 4th edition, by Bauer, Arndt, Gingrich, Danker, 1958. See also Ephesians 2:20 where Paul writes "You are fellow citizens with the saints, and are of God's household, having been built on the foundation of the apostles and prophets, Christ Jesus himself being the corner stone." To put it another way, the ministry of the apostles and prophets during the time NT scripture was being formulated provided the foundation on which all Christian theology and truth stands. Their teaching was all about Christ and His work in and through the church. He is still primary today (the foundation still stands!), not a human representative.

[122] Metzger, 254.

[123] Carson and Moo, 736-37.

[124] Paul set a precedent of looking to the generally held beliefs or practices of the churches (see 1 Corinthians 1:16).

[125] Carson and Moo, 733, relying on the research of John Barton, *Holy Writings, Sacred Text: The Canon in Early Christianity* (Louisville1997: Westminster John Knox, 1997).

[126] Bruce, *The Canon of Scripture*, 150.

[127] In fact, even the apostolic writings themselves raise this awareness. See Galatians 1:8-9, Colossians 2:8, etc.

[128] Metzger, 119.

[129] Ibid. 114.

[130] See Metzger, 130.

[131] Christianity originated in the east, but moved west to Rome and beyond.

[132] Gamble accepts that Justin Martyr held the gospel accounts according to Matthew, Luke and probably Mark to be apostolic in origin. (Gamble, 28-29). But, he goes on to say that Justin does not regard them as canonical. However, the concept of "canon" as a collected set of officially designated authoritative books had not yet been fully developed during Justin's time. Yet, Justin certainly provides evidence that these three gospel accounts were certainly held as authoritative.

[133] Polycarp was probably a disciple of the apostle, though some dispute that he was a disciple of another "John."

[134] Bruce, *The Canon of Scripture*, 171-72. While Irenaeus' writings have been used to support the later doctrine of apostolic succession, with which we disagree, we do note that Irenaeus addresses the weight given to those churches which could in fact trace their orthodoxy more directly back to one or more apostles.

[135] Irenaeus also included the Shepherd of Hermas, though it is questionable whether he considered this book on the same level as the others. What is significant is that he clearly delineated a list of authoritative books separate from all others.

[136] Concurrently, the OT was translated from the Septuagint (see below) into Latin. Later, Jerome produced a complete new translation from the Hebrew OT into Latin. Ibid, 83.

[137] Ibid. 177-78.

[138] Bruce, *The Canon of Scripture*, 181.

[139] At this time, the Christian faith was already planted in India and the church in Egypt had been strongly influenced by Gnosticism.

[140] Ibid. 188.

[141] Bruce, *The Canon of Scripture*, 93. "[Jerome] and Origen stand alone among early church Fathers for their expertise as biblical scholars; of the two, Jerome exercised the greater and more long-lasting influence." See Ibid. 94 for an interesting description of the discussions between Jerome and Augustine about translating the OT from Hebrew versus translating from the Greek Septuagint.

[142] Carson and Moo, 732.

[143] Dunbar, 317.

144 It is important to point out that not all the eastern churches settled on the same Canon as that accepted in the west. Even today some churches descended from them reject some books like Revelation, while others accept additional books (Ibid. 735).

145 NT historian Bruce comments about Eusebius' historical acumen, "Eusebius was deficient in some of the critical qualities requisite in a first-class historian, but he knew the importance of consulting primary sources, and indeed he introduces frequent quotations from them. We have to thank him for preserving portions of ancient writings (such as Papias's) which would otherwise be quite lost to us." (Bruce, *The Canon of Scripture*, 198).

146 Bruce, *The Canon of Scripture*, 203-04. Bruce believes the 50 copies produced by Eusebius were based on the text type that became the ancestor to the so-called "Majority Text" which would explain the MT's popularity through history (also called the Byzantine Text).

147 Other witnesses to a developing list of authoritative books can be found in the Sixtieth Synod of Laodicea (AD 367) which included a catalog of our present twenty-seven books except the Revelation, and the Third Council of Carthage (AD 397 and confirmed again in 419) which prescribed the current twenty-seven books of the NT. Augustine was present at both councils and his views were probably decisive for the definition of the Canon. (Dunbar, 317).

148 "In Syria the usage of the churches at the end of the fourth and beginning of the fifth centuries is indicated by the Peshitta version, which includes twenty-two New Testament books (omitting 2 Peter, 2 and 3 John, Jude, and the Apocalypse) . . . Outside the sphere of Syrian influence there was growing acceptance for all seven of the Catholic Epistles, while doubts still remained with many on the authenticity of the Apocalypse. Yet even in regard to the latter book there were voices of acceptance in different quarters." (Dunbar, 317).

149 Interestingly, Eusebius himself denied the authenticity of James, 2 Peter and Jude, yet he included these in his canon while noting their disputed status. Eventually, however, the three were seen as authoritative.

150 Carson and Moo, 735.

151 Metzger, 75.

CHAPTER 9
THE NON-CANONICAL WRITINGS

152 Roman Catholicism prefers to use the term "deutero-canonical" to emphasis that these books are part of a "second" canon, and thus carrying some measure of authority.

¹⁵³ By "legend" we mean that the ancient writers, who give evidence of how the Septuagint came into being do not cite hard, factual details, but rely on what was thought to be the case.

¹⁵⁴ The astute reader will recognize the obvious—that though the legend speaks of "72", the term "LXX" is the Latin number 70. Such is the stuff of legends!

¹⁵⁵ Bruce, *The Canon of Scripture*, 96.

¹⁵⁶ As Bruce points out, the proceedings of the council at Hippo have been lost to us, but they were summarized in the Council of Carthage in 397. Ibid, 97.

¹⁵⁷ See Carson and Moo, 730.

¹⁵⁸ Of interest, the common Roman Catholic practice of praying for the dead is found in the apocryphal book of 2 Maccabbees in 12:45f, but is nowhere found in the twenty-seven books of the NT. As history demonstrates, the reaction to praying for the dead was very prominent in the start of the protestant reformation.

¹⁵⁹ The abbreviation AV, which stands for "The Authorized Version," is interchangeable, for all intents and purposes, with KJV ("King James Version").

¹⁶⁰ See the preface to the NET Apocrypha Bible.

¹⁶¹ Council of Trent, Session 4, April 1546. See *www.ewtn.com/library/councils/trent4.htm*.

¹⁶² Bruce, *The Canon of Scripture*, 105. The term "deuterocanonical" means second or lesser canon and is meant to distinguish the apocrypha from that which is "canonical." While there is a distinction maintained between the accepted Canon of the NT and the Apocrypha, the debate continues as to the nature of that difference. What is significant is the universal acknowledgment of a difference.

¹⁶³ See "Questions and Answers," *www.bible.org/qa.php?qa_id=147&topic_id=7*

¹⁶⁴ Yet, as David G. Dunbar points out, some protestant scholars today are challenging the Reformers' rejection of the canonicity of the Apocrypha. David G. Dunbar, "The Biblical Canon," chapter 9, in *Hermeneutics, Authority and Canon*, D. A. Carson and John D. Woodbridge, eds. (Eugene, OR: Wipf & Stock Publishers, 2005), 117-121.

¹⁶⁵ For a more complete description of the apocryphal books, see Paul D. Wegner, *The Journey From Text To Translations: The Origin and Development of the Bible* (Grand Rapids, MI: Baker Book House, 1999), 120-123.

166 Wegner, 124. See Metzger 158-173 for a listing of allusions in the NT writings to apocryphal books. Even if there were such direct quotes from the Apocrypha, we note that Paul also made direct quotes from other non-canonical books (see 1 Corinthians 15:33 where Paul quotes from a Greek poet Menander, or Jude 14 and 15 which quotes from 1 Enoch 1:9, a spurious book current at that time). Quoting a book or not quoting a book, therefore, does not determine its canonicity.

167 For an excellent list of inaccuracies in the apocryphal books see Wegner, 125.

168 Another word used by scholars is "spurious."

169 Metzger, 169.

170 Ibid. 174.

171 Interestingly, a careful comparison of the book of Acts and Paul's biblical writings to the believers in Corinth, suggests that the apostle wrote at least four letters to the Corinthian believers, of which we have his second and fourth letters (named 1 and 2 Corinthians). Neither of these missing letters could be the one written in AD 170, obviously because Paul would have been long dead by the time of its composition.

172 See descriptions of these earlier in this book.

173 Interestingly, in 1st Clement 42-45 we have for the first time a reasoned theological argument for dividing the Christian community between "the clergy" and "the laity."

174 Dunbar, 329.

CHAPTER 10
CANON AND CHURCH AUTHORITY

175 Quoted in David G. Dunbar, "The Biblical Canon," chapter 9, in *Hermeneutics, Authority and Canon*, D. A. Carson and John D. Woodbridge, eds. (Eugene, OR: Wipf & Stock Publishers, 2005), 351.

176 Ibid. 352.

177 Ibid. 356.

178 Ibid. 357-358.

179 Quoted in ibid. 355.

180 See ibid. 353.

Chapter 11
Formatting the Texts

[181] Wegner, 213.

[182] The Greek word for gospel, *euangelion*, literally means "good news."

[183] The Pentateuch is the term given to the first five books of the Hebrew OT. Another name for these is "The Book of the Law" or simply "The Law." The Law is comprised of: Genesis, Exodus, Leviticus, Numbers, Deuteronomy. Other common classifications of OT books are: The Historical Books (Joshua through Esther), the Poetic Books (Job, Psalms, Proverbs, Ecclesiastes, Song of Solomon) and the Prophets (major and minor).

[184] Metzger, 296.

[185] The author of "James" was not the apostle James who was martyred (Acts 12) long before this epistle was written. He is most likely the half-brother of Jesus.

[186] We note here that Paul's letters, though occasioned by the specific needs in individual churches, were none-the-less authoritative for all Christians. See 1 Corinthians 1:1-2 were Paul is addressing the Corinthians who are identified ". . . with all who in every place call on the name of our Lord Jesus Christ . . ."

Chapter 12
Putting It All Together

[187] It is interesting that in his voluminous writings, Paul never attempted a biography of Christ as did the four gospel writers.

[188] Carson and Moo, 737.

[189] Dr. Norman Geisler, class notes, "Bibliology," Dallas Seminary, 1979.

[190] Some people quote Revelation 22:18 as proof that the Canon is closed ("I testify to everyone who hears the words of the prophecy of this book: if anyone adds to them, God will add to him the plagues which are written in this book"). However, in context, the warning refers to the book of the Revelation of Jesus Christ and not necessarily to the entire NT.

Chapter 14
Conclusion

[191] For a fuller treatment of the subject matter of this book, the reader is encouraged to consult the excellent resources listed in the annotated bibliography, to which this writer is greatly indebted.